Broadway Christian Chur
Blessed Assurance As Reveale
Newell, Arlo F.

P9-DBS-469

0000 0609

Blessed Assurance

as
Revealed in
Scripture

by
Arlo F. Newell

PROPERTY OF
BROADWAY CHRISTIAN CHURCH LIBRARY
910 BROADWAY
FORT WAYNE, IN 46802

All Scripture quotations in this publication, unless otherwise noted, are from the Holy Bible, New International Version. Copyright ©1973, 1978, International Bible Society. Used by permission of Zondervan Bible Publishers.

All italics in Scripture quotations show emphasis of the author, unless otherwise noted.

Copyright ©1987 by
Warner Press, Inc.
ISBN: 0-87162-480-X

Dedicated

to

Christian pilgrims who dare
to deal honestly with questions
of faith, bearing witness to
the blessed assurance that God
is establishing us in the truth
of his Word.

Contents

Introduction:

Two different events have prodded me on in the writing of this small book. One was during a preaching assignment in Wise, Virginia, with my good friend, Leon Hartwig. Each evening a young man from the local community college attended the services. His interest was obvious. Then, after a sermon on biblical beliefs, he stopped to speak to me at the door with this comment: "I am so glad to hear someone your age state what he believes."

He was attempting to be complimentary but at the same time I felt a sense of embarrassment. I was embarrassed by the fact that there have been times when those of us who are a bit older have failed to speak out or live out our faith. What do we believe? What are those deep, abiding convictions that govern our lives? Are absolutes obsolete? Were they ever absolute?

My young friend was not asking for a plastic faith—brittle and breakable. But he was seeking for some certitudes in life that would enable

1

him to know the boundaries that give some semblance of sanity to a struggling society. Therefore, I was made to take an inventory of my life as to what type of security I have in Christ. What did I really believe?

Out of this frustration I was thrust into a deeper self-search by reading the book *The Myth of Certainty* by Daniel Taylor. So many of the things stated in his provocative writing resonated with my own quest for a reasonable faith. While having certain fixed concepts of faith, I believe that to be Christian means to grow in the grace and knowledge of our Lord and Savior Jesus Christ. One must be open to struggling with the great issues of faith as they impact life, death, and eternity.

When dealing with such issues I am frustrated with the smugness of some saints(?) who seem to have a pat answer, spouting proof texts that address my present developmental dilemma. It is out of the difficult days of my pilgrimage that the greatest discoveries have been made, realizing that there are certitudes in life, assurances of God's steadfast love as we seek to learn of him.

Of major importance to my personal faith was the discovery that doubting can pay divine dividends. Thomas was not cut off because he had the courage to want to see and feel for himself. Rather than taking what others said, becoming a Christian clone, he was honest enough to state up front that he really wanted to know that Christ was alive. We do not always allow others to make that discovery.

The dividend of doubting is that you discover

for yourself an authentic faith. Your faith goes far beyond a group of memorized proof texts; you have personally met the Christ. Now, with Paul you can say, "I know whom I have believed" (2 Tim. 1:12). It is this type of struggle of the soul, not doctrines or church decrees, that makes one fully persuaded.

For that very reason I have attempted to address those common, universal assurances that may be *experienced* by every believer in Christ. To do so does not ignore historic Christian teachings; but it is hoped that by focusing on these promises of God, one may rise above the skepticism that is so apparent in today's culture.

Confession must be made at the point of being tempted to retreat into the security of the past. There was a time when as a child of God I thought there was a pat answer for every problem. All the way from world conflict to abortion to equal rights, there was one simple answer: I believe the Bible.

But the honesty demanded in biblical studies and the integrity required in the interpretation of Scripture placed me in the midst of theological turmoil. While believing in the fundamentals of the Christian faith, I am not what you would call a fundamentalist. Nor would the avant-garde liberals care to have such a conservative listed as one of their following. Therefore, if the quest was to be honest and intellectually credible, then it must address those biblical assurances revealed in Scripture that would apply to all persons in the full spectrum of our spiritual pilgrimage.

3

Some will jump to conclusions at this point, assuming that if the assurances addressed can be believed by everyone, then they will probably be so bland that they have no substance. It will appear to some as a compromise of convictions, allowing for the erosion of our faith rather than building upon the solid foundation of divinely inspired and revealed truth.

It is because of this that the writer is tempted to withdraw into the fetal position of faith, wrapped in the warmth and security of that first innocent faith experience. But no child ever came into the world without the passage from safe security into the stark, struggling existence of development.

All that I have discovered in my seeking after God has confirmed my belief that Scripture is a progressive revelation of God and that to know him, one must grow in grace and knowledge. There is no stopping place in this development of faith. Doubting is not a curse, it is often a blessing in disguise, planting within us the desire for knowing and experiencing God. Only in knowing him are we equipped to make critical judgments on the essential and nonessential, those things or ideas that are of God or humanity.

While Scripture is divinely inspired, it is also lived out in a very human world. The covenant of faith cannot be separated from the community of faith and the culture that surrounds it. Christian faith is called upon to address some very profound cultural problems. The demand placed upon faith has sometimes defeated well-meaning persons who, because there seemed to be no absolute certainties, gave up the faith.

For such persons I hope this small volume will help them to reach once again for a faith founded on the blessed assurance of the Book: a faith that is not taking sides with Athens or Jerusalem—intellectualism or religion—but a synthesis of the two as they are joined in dialogue built upon assurances that transcend individual interpretation or revelation; the blessed assurance authenticated by the constancy of God and those universal graces provided by his beneficence; a faith that is not contrived, adjusting to our culture, but a faith that continues to grow as you live with the blessed assurance that Jesus Christ lives within your heart.

—Arlo F. Newell

Blessed Assurance

Blessed assurance, Jesus is mine!
   Oh, what a foretaste of glory divine!
Heir of salvation purchase of God,
   Born of his Spirit, washed in his blood.

Perfect submission, perfect delight,
   Visions of rapture now burst on my sight;
Angels descending, bring from above
   Echoes of mercy, whispers of love.

Perfect submission, all is at rest,
   I in my Savior am happy and blest;
Watching and waiting, looking above,
   Filled with his goodness, lost in his love.

This is my story, this is my song,
   Praising my Savior all the day long;
This is my story, this is my song,
   Praising my Savior all the day long.
            —Fanny J. Crosby

Hymnal of the Church of God, no. 315

Chapter 1
You Can Be Sure!

Therefore, brothers, since we have confidence to enter the Most Holy Place by the blood of Jesus, by a new and living way opened for us through the curtain, that is, his body, and since we have a great high priest over the house of God, let us draw near to God with a sincere heart in full assurance of faith, having our hearts sprinkled to cleanse us from a guilty conscience and having our bodies washed with pure water. Let us hold unswervingly to the hope we profess, for he who promised is faithful.

—Hebrews 10:19-23

Teach Me Thy Way

Teach me thy Way, O Lord, Teach me thy Way!
  Thy guiding grace afford—Teach me thy Way!
Help me to walk aright, More by faith, less by sight;
  Lead me with heavenly light—Teach me thy Way!
When I am sad at heart, Teach me thy Way!
  When earthly joys depart, Teach me thy Way!
In hours of loneliness, In times of dire distress,
  In failure or success, Teach me thy Way!
When doubts and fears arise, Teach me thy Way!
  When storms o'er-spread the skies, Teach
  me thy Way!
Shine through the cloud and rain, Through sorrow,
  toil and pain;
  Make thou my pathway plain—Teach me thy Way!
Long as my life shall last, Teach me thy Way!
  Where'er my lot be cast, Teach me thy Way!
Until the race is run, Until the journey's done,
  Until the crown is won, Teach me thy Way!
Amen.

—B. Mansell Ramsey

Hymnal of the Church of God, no. 385

The statement was positive, affirming, and encouraging. It helped to stabilize my spiritual life when severe storms of doubt and disbelief sought to destroy it. The simple faith of my childhood—those truths so often taken for granted because of what others believed—had been shattered by a world that knew not God or his Word. My eyes had been opened to behold the human inconsistencies that so often accompany our claim to Christian faith. There was disparagement between deed and disposition, between action and attitude, between flesh and spirit.

Trying to understand was becoming more than I could handle as my own life came up before me in serious thought. It seemed that, like Paul, I did "not understand what I do. For what I want to do I do not do, but what I hate I do" (Rom. 7:15). Maybe the world was right—

there is no real victory over sin and self. Why not just go along with the crowd, eat, drink, and be merry, and forget about this idea of holiness, happiness, and heaven.

But into that turbulent time in my life came this ray of hope shining through the darkness. No, it was not some grand theological statement of historical Christianity. Nor was it a doctrinal declaration of orthodoxy from the institutional church. It wasn't even an emotional experience prompted by the televangelist in a mass meeting.

What was the statement? It was the word of an ordinary person, a friend and pilgrim in the Christian way, someone just like me. As I openly shared my personal quest about God, the humanness of the Church, and the desire to truly live for Christ, my friend said, *"You can be sure. . . ."*

I don't remember all the other things that were said, but what was needed most had already been communicated. The Holy Spirit had taken these simple words of an unordained, ordinary Christian who had discovered that you can be sure about your faith and about your relationship with Christ. This assurance is not dependent on what you do but on what Christ has done for you—an assurance that is based not on your performance but upon his precious promises in the Word of God. Yes, you can be sure!

This personal pilgrimage is not unlike that addressed by the writer of Hebrews. A preacher with a pastor's heart helps a persecuted and scattered people to know the assurance of God's presence, provision, and power. They are assured that in the midst of a pagan world, he has provided a great salvation that is able to save to the uttermost all those who trust in him.

With intense passion and persistence the preacher urges the reader to hear this God who speaks. The God who spoke in the past addresses us in the present and calls us into the future. It is this blessed assurance of full salvation and his continuing presence that the passage promises.

Such assurance does not diminish the cost of discipleship or the possibility of persecution or personal suffering. Nor does it eliminate the temptation to apathy, indifference, or neglect in spiritual discipline. The preacher attempts to help the followers of Christ to know, with confidence, that even in the face of martyrdom, Christ is with them and will never forsake them.

Only in Christ is such assurance possible—the assurance that you are saved, that your sins are forgiven, and that your name has been recorded in the Lamb's Book of Life. This is an assurance upon which you can depend when your feelings are at their lowest ebb and when your faith falters.

That blessed assurance does not come as a result of years of experience or from academic training. Crisis in Christian experience comes to all of us and at every stage in our pilgrimage as the people of God. The crisis overwhelms you and you have no answers.

Personal questions arise such as, If I'm really saved, why do I feel so bad? You face questions about the inequities of life: In a world of plenty, why does God allow people to starve? or, Why do Christians, living faithfully for God, suffer physically or fail financially?

Answers to questions like these and others do not come from pat answers or proof texts of Scripture but from One who has penetrated our human predicament and provided solutions to our problems. It is this assurance that we lift up in this chapter.

Authenticate Your Faith in Jesus Christ

The incarnation authenticates this assurance from God's Word. It is the Word become flesh (John 1:14) that helps us to reach out and claim what Christ has accomplished for all who trust him. Within all of us is the desire to find someone to help us, someone who has experienced what we are experiencing.

At a time of physical suffering within our own family, we reached out not to theorists who could tell us all about the physical problems—what we wanted and needed was the authentic testimony of someone who had been through the struggle. We needed someone who had suffered as we were suffering. We wanted more than someone who said, "I understand." We wanted someone who could say, "I have been there before you."

Because of this desire for a friend who has endured the pain, the suffering, and/or sorrow, the preacher of Hebrews includes this assurance: "We do not have a high priest who is unable to sympathize with our weaknesses, but we have one who was tempted in every way, just as we are—yet was without sin" (4:15). Each time I read that passage I am assured that there is not a single temptation confronting me that Jesus has not already conquered. He fully understands my human desires, hungers, and drives because he became like me.

Appropriate Assurance by Trusting God

To appropriate this assurance it is essential that I come to trust God implicitly. The foundation of such a faith is the awareness that Christ is compassionate in his relationship with us. "God made him who had no sin to be sin for us, so that in him we might become the righteousness of God" (2 Cor. 5:21).

In the wilderness Jesus was tempted. In the garden he revealed his sensitive spirit as he prayed, "If it is possible, may this cup be taken from me. Yet not as I will, but as you will" (Matt. 26:39).

This compassionate Christ who has endured human suffering helps us to trust God completely. Only a God who is so faithful to his people is deserving and worthy of our confidence, our trust.

This trust enables us to come "boldly" to the throne of grace, seeking help unashamedly in time of personal need. We are not beggars! We are children of the King with immediate access to all the resources of heaven. Christ, as our High Priest, has provided a "way," an entrance into his presence. Through him we have access to the One who has all power, dominion, wisdom, authority, and glory. Christ authenticates this blessed assurance and our trust in God enables us to appropriate his grace.

Assimilate This Assurance in Your Daily Life

When confronted by conflict or when struggling with suffering, our major concern is about how we assimilate this assurance for our present, personal need. The preacher in Hebrews not only affirms that "You can be sure . . . " but that you can assimilate confidence into your daily life. Decision and discipline are essentials in Christian assurance.

While the Holy Spirit draws me to God, he will not draw me against my will. If I want assurance in my Christian life it is necessary that I willfully assimilate and take advantage of my opportunity to receive what God has provided.

Drawing near to God strengthens the divine/human relationship and increases one's faith. Such intimacy is possible through the full assurance that Christ has provided the "way" and God will not reject those whom the Son has cleansed. The genuineness and reality of our assurance are indicated by this act of drawing near to God. These leave no question as to where we have found our assurance for living.

An older saint told of his struggles to find faith in God. He debated often with his doubts, finally coming to the discovery that "the important question became not whether I thought

God was real, but whether God thought I was real." Drawing near indicates *my* trust in God and *my* obedience to his will.

While drawing near to God may be done in the privacy of my own personal life, it is the "profession" or "confession" of this faith in public that develops my spiritual strength. Those to whom the preacher spoke were being tempted to withdraw into the accepted religious ritual of the day rather than to "profess" openly and unashamedly their faith in God. They are encouraged to hold fast, unswervingly, tightening down, securing their faith in God's power to save and keep.

You can be sure that God will not fail. His promises are true because he stands behind each one. When the pressure of public opinion and the contrary winds of doctrinal differences blow about you, "hold unswervingly to the hope we profess, for he who promised is faithful."

As a final directive to assimilating this blessed assurance, the preacher says, "Let us consider one another." Draw near to God, hold fast your profession of faith, and now, "consider one another." Assurance comes from my personal nearness to God, it is strengthened by my public profession of faith, and it is extended by practical relationship with people. The blessed assurance revealed in Scripture is always in the context of the covenant community. It is the happy assurance of interdependency within the body of Christ, the community of faith, the Church.

Yes, you can be sure that Christ has saved you to the uttermost because he alone can authenticate your experience. He became like you, suffered and died for you, making possible your redemption. You can be sure because you appropriate his grace through faith that trusts him completely. Faith is interrelational. We must believe in God and his Son, Jesus Christ, not in creeds and disciplines. And finally, you can be sure because you have come to assimilate this blessed assurance by your personally drawing near to God, by publicly professing the lordship of Christ, and in your practical participation with the people of God. To strengthen your grasp on this blessed assurance, take time to review the Scripture lesson, then set about memorizing these selected verses.

Blessed Assurance
As Revealed in Scripture
Chapter 1
You Can Be Sure!

Assurance of Being God's Children
John 1:12-13

To all who received him, to those who *believed in his name*, he gave the right to become children of God—children born not of natural descent, nor of human decision or a husband's will, but born of God.

1 John 3:2

Now we are children of God, and what we will be has not yet been made known. But *we know* that when he appears, we shall be like him, for we shall see him as he is.

Assurance of His Keeping Power
2 Timothy 1:12

I know whom I have believed, and *am convinced* that *he is able* to guard what I have entrusted to him for that day.

Assurance of Knowing Christ
Colossians 2:2-3, Living Bible

This is what I have asked of God for you: that you will be encouraged and knit together by strong ties of love, and that you will have the rich experience of *knowing Christ with real certainty and clear understanding*. For God's secret plan, now at last made known, is Christ himself. In him lie hidden all the mighty untapped treasures of wisdom and knowledge.

Assurance of Access to God
Hebrews 10:22-23
Let us draw near to God with a sincere heart in *full assurance of faith*, having our hearts sprinkled to cleanse us from a guilty conscience and having our bodies washed with pure water. Let us hold unswervingly to the hope we profess, for he who promised is faithful.

Chapter 2
God Is!

If ... you seek the Lord your God, you will find him if you look for him with all your heart and with all your soul.
—**Deuteronomy 4:29**

And without faith it is impossible to please God, because anyone who comes to him must believe that he exists and that he rewards those who earnestly seek him.
—**Hebrews 11:6**

There's a Wideness in God's Mercy

There's a wideness in God's mercy,
  Like the wideness of the sea;
There's a kindness in his justice,
  Which is more than liberty.

For the love of God is broader
  Than the measure of man's mind;
And the heart of the Eternal
  Is most wonderfully kind.

There is plentiful redemption
  In the blood that has been shed;
There is joy for all the members
  In the sorrows of the Head.

If our love were but more simple,
  We should take him at his word;
And our lives would be all sunshine
  In the sweetness of our Lord.
Amen.
        —Frederick W. Faber

Hymnal of the Church of God, no. 37

PROPERTY OF
BROADWAY CHRISTIAN CHURCH LIBRARY
910 BROADWAY
FORT WAYNE, IN 46802

Job believed in God. But like many of us he didn't really understand God and many times seriously questioned God's judgments. Job wanted some assurance about where God was and why God allowed certain things to happen. It is a very human picture conjured by Job's plea, "If only I knew where to find him ... I would state my case before him and fill my mouth with arguments" (Job 23:3-4).

Out of his loss of family, possessions, and reputation, Job discovered not patience *but God.* Most assuredly Job demonstrated patient endurance when confronted by tragedy, physical suffering, and emotional trauma, but paramount in the account is the radiant *reality that God is*— and the discovery was made in the midst of the storm.

Visiting the doctor's office for an allergy checkup, I observed the many patients awaiting the hour of their appointments. There were mothers with feverish children, older people faced by failing health, and many others needing physical care. All of us were keenly aware of the stress produced by sickness.

Then, on the counter I noticed a small plaque that read, "Sometimes God stills the storm and at other times He stills me in the midst of the storm." That is where Job discovered the reality of God—in the midst of the storm (see 40:6).

How many times have we questioned the reality of God because of our circumstances—circumstances over which we seemingly have very little control? Such circumstances, however, bring forth in us the agony of honesty, that point in our personal faith development at which we openly confess, "I just don't know."

We long for the assurance that we know the final word because of our "hot line to heaven," but deep down in our hearts and in the integrity of our minds we know there are questions yet unanswered. Before I can give positive proof texts about nuclear warfare, abortion, AIDS, and homosexuality, I must have some assurance about God.

God is most often discovered in the dark and difficult days of our personal pilgrimage. Only then, when in the midst of life's mystery and misery, do we truly seek God. It was in the distressing experience of exile from home, security, and religious surroundings that Israel received the assurance, "If . . . you seek the Lord your God, you will find him if you look for him with all your heart and with all your soul" (Deut. 4:29).

God does not change! (See Malachi 3:6.) He is reliable and his laws are immutable. Herein do we find security as we grasp desperately for straws. Surprisingly, in our moments of deep insecurity we now find that which is eternal and everlasting. But if we are to find, we must seek for God with our *whole* being!

This is not a superficial, cosmetic Christian profession that sees us only through the good times as we ride the crest of popular opinion, but a deep, abiding faith in the living God that sustains us when there are no reasonable, rational answers to life and death.

The assurance we are looking for is that this God of Abraham, Isaac, and Jacob will be *our* God and when we seek for him with all our being he will be there and hear our cry. It is the security born of simple trust, like that of a child believing the parent is always there and is always adequate for the situation.

God was here before we arrived, his divine power and presence have been manifest in salvation history across the years, and he will be there in the future when we reach out for him. "He that cometh to God must believe that he is" is not a mere intellectual assent but an interpersonal relationship that is born of personal trust.

Sharon Parker, in her book *The Critical Years*, calls our attention to a film made during the last years of the life of famed psychiatrist Carl Jung. In the film, Dr. Jung is asked by an interviewer, "Do you believe in God?" Jung immediately replied, "No."

Some of the audience was heard to laugh, thinking that the statement indicated that Jung was too sophisticated to believe in God. But then the greatness of Carl Jung came forth as he added, "I don't have to believe in God—*I know God*."

The God of the Bible Is Knowable

It appears overly simplified in our quest for God for someone to say that we can know God as a friend. This creator of the universe, who brought the galaxies into being, called the stars by name and charted the courses of the seas, One who is all powerful, able to arrange the atoms, control the elements, and bring into being the miracle of the human mind—such a God has chosen to reveal himself to us in terms we understand. (See Romans 1:19.) And the language chosen is that which we most readily comprehend, the language of relationship.

Therefore, the earliest accounts of Genesis do not begin with theological theories of interpretation but with simple stories of friendship. It is the portrayal of this Creator God as he walked and talked with Adam and Eve in the garden. Such terms are sometimes referred to as anthropomorphic, meaning to be related to human form or concept.

Though the idea is frowned upon by some scholars, one's assurance of faith in God can be greatly enhanced by viewing him as a friend—a friend, who, like C. Austin Miles wrote in 1912, "walks with me, and talks with me, and tells me I am his own." This beloved gospel song is more than mere emotional sentimentalism; it is the assurance that the God of the Bible is knowable and by faith we can experience this divine/human relationship.

The God of History Is Reliable

Those persons referred to in Hebrews, chapter eleven, were real people. History bears witness to their family connections, their contributions to culture, and their continuing faith in God. Whatever confronted them in life, they believed that Israel's God would provide for them.

To be assured of the reliability they placed in God, one needs only to read the account of their deliverance and the way God cared for them through the wilderness. It has become a part of Jewish tradition to recount the manner in which God was able to meet their needs. "We cried out to the Lord . . . the Lord heard our voice and saw our misery . . . the Lord brought us out of Egypt . . . and gave us this land . . . flowing with milk and honey" (Deut. 26:5-9). In the midst of their frequent grumbling, disobedience, and backslidings, they knew that when they reached out by faith, they had the assurance of God's covenant that he would respond to their cry.

Beyond the physical needs of a people calling on God, there is the assurance that God is reliable for every area of need in the lives of his children. The writer of Proverbs underscores what trusting will bring to pass. "Trust in the Lord with all your heart and lean not to your own understanding; in all your ways acknowl-

edge him, and he will make your paths straight"
(3:5-6).

What glorious assurance is available for those
who are willing simply to *trust* God, but such
trust does require that we trust *with all our
heart* and acknowledge him in *all our ways*. To
do so does not allow for *leaning on our own
understanding* but insists that we completely
trust in God's reliability. There is not a decision
we make—choice of friends or a marriage part-
ner, business decisions, future plans—that this
God of history is not able and willing to help if
we will place our trust in him. History and the
Bible assure us that God is knowable and reliable—we can count on him.

The God of Might Is Accessible

Reverence is a meaningful word throughout
Scripture. It is the recognition given to the
power and position of one in authority, usually
reserved for kings, strong and mighty. The
psalmist wrote, "The fear [reverence] of the
Lord is the beginning of wisdom" (111:10).

But because of the greatness of the King and
our reverence, we sometimes become fearful of
approaching him; he becomes inaccessible. The
Ruler is out of touch with our human situation
of ordinary living. It is this type of fear or
reverence that makes it necessary to have the
assurance that whenever we cry unto the Lord,
he is always accessible. God always hears our
cry!

God's hearing is not predicated or based on
what you have done, how much you have given,
or where you are when you call. Very plainly

the psalmist states his confession: "This poor man called, and the Lord heard him; he saved him out of all his troubles" (34:6).

It is also the psalmist who puts God on a constant-call basis. You are assured that whenever you call, day or night, all of the resources of heaven are available to you. "He will not let your foot slip—he who watches over you will not slumber; indeed, he who watches over Israel will neither slumber nor sleep" (121:3-4).

Because such assurances seemed too good to be true, the Word of God carried the prophecy of this God coming to dwell with us. When Christ was to be born, the inspired writer stated, "All this took place to fulfill what the Lord had said through the prophet: 'The virgin will be with child and will give birth to a son, and they will call him Immanuel'—which means, *'God with us'* " (Matt. 1:23).

We are assured by Scripture, by history, and by his divine presence that we can know God. He is accessible and desires that we come to have that confidence in our personal experience. God is here—expressing himself in love for all people as he seeks to save and to serve. You can be sure that this God, revealed in Christ, is your Lord and Savior.

Blessed Assurance
As Revealed in Scripture
Chapter 2
God Is!

Assurance of One God
Exodus 20:2-3
I am the Lord your God ... You shall have *no other gods before me.*
Deuteronomy 6:4
Hear, O Israel: The Lord our God, *the Lord is one.* Love the Lord your God with all your heart and with all your soul and with all your strength.
Isaiah 45:22
Turn to me and be saved, all you ends of the earth; for *I am God, and there is no other.*
1 Corinthians 8:6
For us there is but *one God*, the Father, from whom all things came and for whom we live; and there is but one Lord, Jesus Christ, through whom all things came and through whom we live.

Assurance of God's Nature
John 4:24
God is spirit, and his worshipers must worship in spirit and in truth.
1 John 1:5
This is the message we have heard from him and declare to you: *God is light*; in him there is no darkness at all.

1 John 4:8
Whoever does not love does not know God, because *God is love.*

1 John 4:16
And so we know and rely on the love God has for us. *God is love.* Whoever lives in love lives in God, and God in him.

Assurance of God's Revelation in Christ

Matthew 1:23
The virgin will be with child and will give birth to a son, and they will call him Immanuel—which means, *"God with us."*

John 17:3
Now this is eternal life: that they may know you, *the only true God,* and Jesus Christ, whom you have sent.

Colossians 1:15, 19
He is *the image of the invisible God,* the first-born over all creation. . . . For God was pleased to *have all his fullness dwell in him.*

Assurance of How to Please God

Hebrews 11:6
And without faith it is impossible *to please God,* because anyone who comes to him must *believe that he exists* and *that he rewards those who earnestly seek him.*

Assurance That God Accepts All People

Acts 10:34-35

Then Peter began to speak: "I now realize how true it is that *God does not show favoritism* but *accepts men from every nation* who fear him and do what is right."

Chapter 3
His Word Is True!

The grass withers and the flowers fall, but the word of our God stands forever.
—Isaiah 40:8

Above all, you must understand that no prophecy of Scripture came about by the prophet's own interpretation. For prophecy never had its origin in the will of man, but men spoke from God as they were carried along by the Holy Spirit.

—2 Peter 1:20-21

How Firm a Foundation

How firm a foundation, ye saints of the Lord,
  Is laid for your faith in his excellent Word!
What more can he say than to you he hath said,
  To you who for refuge to Jesus have fled?

Fear not, I am with thee; O be not dismayed,
  For I am thy God and will still give thee aid;
I'll strengthen thee, help thee, and cause thee
  to stand,
  Upheld by my righteous, omnipotent hand.

When through fiery trials thy pathway shall lie,
  My grace, all sufficient, shall be thy supply;
The flame shall not hurt thee; I only design
  Thy dross to consume, and thy gold to refine.

The soul that on Jesus hath leaned for repose
  I will not, I will not desert to his foes;
That soul, though all hell should endeavor
  to shake,
  I'll never, no, never, no, never forsake!

—"K" in Rippon's "Selection," 1787

Hymnal of the Church of God, no. 430

The Bible is God's inspired Word. I believe it to be completely trustworthy in all matters of faith and practice. Much more than a religious "best seller," it is the one book that brings God's Word to a world of shrinking boundaries and expanding morals, a world in which the faithful and fanatical periodically engage in a battle about the Bible.

What translation is correct? Whose interpretation is to be trusted and accepted as standard? Which side of the issue, conservative or liberal, shall I take? Can we be "evangelical" Christians, united in Christ, without all agreeing on each theological point?

An epidemic of uncertainty has crippled the church. This disease is born of uncertainty about the relevancy, authenticity, and authority of Scripture. The fickleness of our faith is evidenced in our theology of justification by adjustment.

With each new interpretation of Scripture we simply adjust our theology to fit the latest fad, until the honest observer questions our Christian profession of faith. Our attempt to be tolerant of differing faiths has become intolerable to those who seek a solid rock upon which to build their discipleship.

In an attempt to counteract this epidemic, some churches have produced puppets that parrot Bible verses verbatim but know little of the Spirit of truth, while others have allowed a generation of spiritual illiterates to develop who cannot give a responsible reason for the hope they profess.

In such an ambiguous atmosphere, the world listens for some word of assurance. As did one of old they ask, "Is there any word from the Lord?" They seek a word that assures them that, if the foundations be destroyed, truth will rise again. We need truth that is applicable to life and dependable in death.

The assurance that the seeker desires is to be found in God's Word. This chapter will not answer all your questions or resolve the academic debates about the Bible that continue in seminary classes and dormitory rooms. The intent is to acknowledge that many of us are still working through some matters of faith that we do not fully understand, but in all of this we have discovered the blessed assurance that God's Word is true.

Divinity of Expression

George Webster gave us these words: "Praise God for his Word! from its pages *divine* came the light of his love to this poor heart of mine."

There is assurance in the knowledge that the Bible is an expression of divinity, meaning that it has come forth from God. From Genesis to Revelation, Scripture is a progressive revelation of God. One beholds the God of the Bible, expressed in the Book's varied literary forms, as Creator, Redeemer, and King of Kings. The Bible is unique in that no other book conveys so clearly its divine origin.

No attempt is made in Scripture to prove its divine authorship. Just as God provides revelation rather than proof, so is the divine origin of Scripture revealed in the writings of the Book. These stories of faith existed as oral tradition long before the church, and only in the fullness of time were they placed in written form, later to be canonized (accepted by decree of the Church) as the completed Book.

One cannot accurately date the Bible's beginning, for the original manuscripts are not available. Its authenticity is not based upon when first written but by how it has stood the test of time. After all these centuries of which we do have accurate records, the Bible still speaks.

It is true, "The grass withers and the flowers fall, but the word of our God stands forever" (Isa. 40:8). Attempts to ban the Bible, to burn the Book, and to persecute the translators have all failed. As Jesus said, "Heaven and earth will pass away, but my word will never pass away" (Matt. 24:34).

This durability is divinely imparted, not something that is popular for a brief period of time. Scripture refers to this as divine inspiration. Paul declares, "All scripture is God-breathed" (2 Tim. 3:16). Just as God breathed into man and woman the breath of life, so he has inspired human writers to communicate his message of truth.

God is still speaking as he has always been through the ages. The Scriptures say, "In the past God spoke to our forefathers through the prophets at many times and in various ways, but in these last days he has spoken to us by his Son" (Heb. 1:1-2).

Today God speaks through the pages of the Bible and through his divinely called ministers. What is preached is to be "the Word," not the preacher's private interpretation but Scripture as revealed through the Holy Spirit. There is assurance when the Word and the Spirit bear witness to the truth.

Integrity of Exploration

Truth, wherever found, can always stand the most severe scrutiny. God's Word stands secure and is not in need of someone or some group to protect or preserve it. Literary criticism, humanism, or fanatical fundamentalism will not destroy the divinely inspired Word of God.

Integrity of exploration is integral to Christian faith. Now, if our assurance is based upon some personal or private interpretation of Scripture, then we have just cause to fear research and inspection. Too many times we have allowed what I choose to call believer's "barnacles" to attach themselves to the Bible.

A barnacle is a form of marine life that sometimes attaches itself to a ship, never helping or contributing to the forward motion of the vessel but at times hindering the smooth operation of the ship. Periodically the ship must enter dry dock where the barnacles are scraped off, thus allowing the vessel to move more freely in the water.

"Barnacles" on the Bible have created many controversies in the Church, keeping the Old Ship of Zion from sailing smoothly. We lose faith and lose people because we debate (fight!) over nonessentials in our belief about the Bible.

Scripture allows for full exposure to the searchlight of higher education, sound reason, and scientific inspection. Did not Jesus say, "Ask and it will be given to you; seek and you will find; knock and the door will be opened to you. For everyone who asks receives; he who seeks finds; and to him who knocks, the door will be opened" (Matt. 7:7)?

With that statement Jesus destroys the concept of "blind" faith. God desires that we exercise our free will and full intellect in exploring and discovering for ourselves convictions about his inspired Word.

When the text is approached honestly, one will inevitably come to say, "Oh, the depth of the riches of the wisdom and knowledge of God! How unsearchable his judgments, and his paths beyond tracing out! 'Who has known the mind of the Lord? Or who has been his counselor?' 'Who has ever given to God that God should

43

repay him?' For from him and through him and to him are all things. To him be glory forever! Amen" (Rom. 11:33-36).

Simplicity of Explanation

This divinely inspired Word that has been tested by scholars of integrity must also bring assurance to *all* people, not just the learned. Such assurance is found in the awareness that at every level of our human experience the Bible speaks to us. As little children listening to Bible stories, as youth seeking for ideals modeling character, as adults struggling with value systems, and as older adults wanting security in an insecure time of life, the Bible reaches us precisely at our point of need.

Too simple? Not really, because God's Word has always addressed human need among the masses in practical ways: it is not written just to a certain elect or select group. We should be extremely cautious of those who major in signs and wonders through which they understand God to speak only to a select group. While in the Old Testament God speaks to us through prophets, priests, and kings, in the New Testament God has chosen to reveal himself through the person of his Son: "The word became flesh and lived for a while among us . . . full of grace and truth" (John 1:14).

This enfleshment, or incarnation, became the revelation of a simple, servant-oriented lifestyle. In so doing, the Word related to people of every walk of life at a personal level. "The common people heard him gladly," says Mark's Gospel (12:37, KJV).

God's purpose and plan were made plain by the language used and illustrations given. Jesus spoke about birds and flowers, seeds and fish, farmers and fishermen. He told simple stories about a father's love for his son, a shepherd and his sheep, and about houses that stand in the midst of the storm.

While plumbing the depths of knowledge and scaling the heights of wisdom, God's Word, inspired by the Holy Spirit, never loses touch with the human heart and soul. What blessed assurance to know that *"whoever* believes in him shall not perish but have eternal life" (John 3:16).

Universality of Experience

Even the Bible can be packaged for marketing in certain cultural wrappings. This is the accusation placed many times against the missionary enterprise—Christ is always in the image of the country from which the missionary has come. It therefore becomes difficult to find the truth of God's Word in its unencumbered form.

Dietrich Bonhoeffer alluded to this when he wrote, "The real trouble is that the pure Word of Jesus has been overlaid with so much human ballast—burdensome rules and regulations, false hopes and consolation—that it has become extremely difficult to make a *genuine* decision for Christ."

We need the assurance that God's Word is true because it teaches a universal experience of salvation. While experienced personally, our faith can be understood universally.

Persons are born very much alike all over the world. Therefore, when the Bible speaks of being "born again," it communicates to every culture. We are born of the Spirit (see John 3:6), as are all who have come to know Christ, and we are a part of a universal family.

While there are many things we may not need to be sure about, it is essential in our Christian pilgrimage that we know what it means to be "born again" as well as what it means to be separated from God.

Sin, therefore, is revealed to us as "death," which is also a universal term. Scripture speaks of being "dead in your transgressions and sin" (Eph. 2:1), and when we are saved, it is as though we have been resurrected to a new life in Christ. Sin, as such, is not just one specific act or deed but is the result of broken relationship with Christ, the giver of Life.

It is because of this universal dimension of the divine Word that when it is presented it penetrates into the personal life of each person who hears. Truth "judges the thoughts and attitudes of the heart" (Heb. 4:12), confronting us with a message that is much greater than any earthly messenger.

Do you have questions about God's Word? Dare to believe and accept the assurance that comes through this divinely revealed truth that has stood the test of time and universally witnesses to a simple, childlike faith in God.

Blessed Assurance

As Revealed in Scripture
Chapter 3
His Word Is True!

Assurance of the Word's Authorship
Psalm 68:11
The Lord announced the word, and great was the company of those who proclaimed it.
Psalm 119:160
All your words are true; all your righteous laws are eternal.
John 1:1
In the beginning was the Word, and the Word was with God, and the Word was God.
2 Timothy 3:16-17
All Scripture is God-breathed and is useful for teaching, rebuking, correcting and training in righteousness, so that the man of God may be thoroughly equipped for every good work.
2 Peter 1:20-21
Above all, you must understand that no prophecy of Scripture came about by the prophet's own interpretation. For prophecy never had its origin in the will of man, but men spoke from God as they were carried along by the Holy Spirit.

Assurance of the Word's Endurance
Isaiah 40:8
The grass withers and the flowers fall, but the word of our God stands forever.
Matthew 24:35
Heaven and earth will pass away, but my words will never pass away.

Assurance of the Word's
Reaching Us
Isaiah 55:11
So . . . my word . . . will not return to me empty,
but will accomplish what I desire and achieve
the purpose for which I sent it.
Hebrews 4:12
The word of God is living and active. Sharper
than any double-edged sword, it penetrates even
to dividing soul and spirit, joints and marrow; it
judges the thoughts and attitudes of the heart.

Assurance of the Word's
Sustaining Us
Matthew 4:4
Man does not live on bread alone, but on every
word that comes from the mouth of God.
1 Peter 2:2-3
Like newborn babies, crave pure spiritual milk
[of the Word], so that by it you may grow up in
your salvation, now that you have tasted that
the Lord is good.

Assurance of the Word
Revealed in Christ
John 1:14
The Word became flesh and lived for a while
among us.

Assurance of the Word's
Dispelling Darkness
Psalm 119:105
Your word is a lamp to my feet and a light for
my path.

John 8:12
When Jesus spoke again to the people, he said,
"I am the light of the world. Whoever follows
me will never walk in darkness, but will have
the light of life."

Assurance of Salvation through the Word
Romans 10:17
Faith comes from hearing the message, and the
message is heard through the word of Christ.
James 1:18
He chose to give us birth through the word of
truth, that we might be a kind of firstfruits of
all he created.
James 1:21-22
Humbly accept the word planted in you, which
can save you. Do not merely listen to the word.
. . . Do what it says.

Assurance of the Word's Power to Keep
Psalm 119:11
I have hidden your word in my heart that I
might not sin against you.

Assurance of the Word for Preaching
2 Timothy 4:2
Preach the Word, be prepared in season and
out of season; correct, rebuke and encourage—
with great patience and careful instruction.

Chapter 4
God's Love Is Everlasting!

The Lord appeared to us in the past, saying: "I have loved you with an everlasting love: I have drawn you with loving-kindness."

—Jeremiah 31:3

We are more than conquerors through him who loved us. For I am convinced that neither death nor life, neither angels nor demons, neither the present nor the future, nor any powers, neither height nor depth, nor anything else in all creation, will be able to separate us from the love of God that is in Christ Jesus our Lord.

—Romans 8:37-39

O Love That Wilt Not Let Me Go

O Love that wilt not let me go,
　I rest my weary soul in thee;
I give thee back the life I owe,
　That in thine ocean depths its flow
May richer, fuller be.

O Light that followest all my way,
　I yield my flickering torch to thee;
My heart restores its borrowed ray,
　That in thy sunshine's blaze its day
May brighter, fairer be.

O Joy that seekest me through pain,
　I cannot close my heart to thee;
I trace the rainbow through the rain,
　And feel the promise is not vain
That morn shall tearless be.

O Cross that liftest up my head,
　I dare not ask to fly from thee;
I lay in dust life's glory dead,
　And from the ground there blossoms red
Life that shall endless be.

Amen.

—George Matheson

Hymnal of the Church of God, no. 398

od loves you! It is an assurance given in his Word that no one can take from you or keep you from accepting. This love is everlasting as is the God of the Bible. "Before the mountains were born or you brought forth the earth and the world, from everlasting to everlasting you are God" (Ps. 90:2).

Nothing, absolutely nothing, can separate you from God's love. In a world of cheap substitutes, this love is like a light that shines, making all others pale in its radiance. God's love accepts the person and rejects the perversion, acknowledges the humanness and accomplishes salvation in Christ. This divine love cannot be equated with human love that manipulates, dominates, and exploits for one's own selfish desires. Revealed in Scripture is the love of God—giving sacrificially, humbly serving and

53

suffering for you as the object of that love—a love that is eternal.

If we could bring together in one moment in history all of the accumulated atrocities of the ages—all of our sinfully selfish, insensitive, inhuman acts and attitudes against God and humankind—that would not change God's love. How tragic that some who have alienated themselves from God's love have been led to believe that their behavior has made God love them less. God's love is understanding of the situation, unchanging in his salvation, and unending in seeking to help persons respond.

Jeremiah reports God saying to his people, "I have loved you with an everlasting love; I have drawn you with loving-kindness" (31:3). This declaration was made to a critical, complaining, backsliding, rebellious people. Because he loved the people of Israel, God had entered into an agreement (covenant) with them. On God's part, there was no turning back—God would forever be faithful, continuing to love the people of Israel regardless of what they did.

This is the same eternal love expressed in Hosea (11:1). God steadfastly determined to be true to his share of the covenant obligation, regardless of what Israel did. Contrary to modern interpretation, it takes two to make a covenant. When common commitment is sealed by love (*chesed*), two persons make the mutual agreement. It is not forced or coerced by outside powers but freely given by personal, willful, decisive action.

Such an agreement also requires two persons to break it. In the Bible, Israel may have rejected God, but God never rejected Israel. At least 245 times in the Old Testament the word *love* (*chesed*) is used to indicate that God persistently seeks the well-being and highest good for his people. In the New Testament the concept is inherent in these words from 1 Corinthians: "Love is patient, love is kind. . . . It always protects, always trusts, always hopes, always perseveres. Love never fails" (13:4, 7, 8).

God has made this covenant to love you forever. Although the word *covenant* is not popular in today's language, it is fundamental to biblical faith. We use it each time we refer to the Old and New Testaments. The word *testament* is only an English form of the Latin, *testamentum*; within the Vulgate it is the rendering used for the Hebrew word *covenant* (*berith*). God's Word, the Bible, is his covenant agreement in which he commits his love to you eternally.

Everlasting Love Reaches Out to Us

There was never a time that God did not love you. Before you were born this Creator God loved and cared for you. As a person with potential for success or failure, God provided for your highest good. And, although you may presently be living in sinful rebellion against his will, God still reaches out to you in love. .

As the Divine Lover, God initiates the action, persistently reaching out to us. His pursuit is not thwarted by our rejection or the slowness of our response. This is portrayed in the words

"When Israel was a child, I *loved* him, and out of Egypt I called my son. But the more I called Israel, the further they went from me. . . . I taught [them] to walk . . . I . . . healed them. . . . I led them with cords of human kindness, with ties of *love*" (Hos. 11:1-4).

This concept is captured in the musical *His Love Reaching*—"His love reached all the way to where I was." Where were you when God's love reached you? In Egyptian bondage, a slave to sin? Wandering in the wilderness, seeking for the Promised Land? Or captured by the modern cultic rites of our hedonistic "happy hour" society?

Regardless of where you were or are, God still reaches out to you in love. Like Francis P. Thompson's *The Hound of Heaven*, relentlessly God seeks you. "For the Son of man is come to seek and to save that which was lost" (Luke 19:10, KJV). Paul wrote, "God commendeth his love toward us, in that, while we were yet sinners, Christ died for us" (Rom. 5:8, KJV). It is a love that does not condemn, for we are condemned already. "For God sent not his Son into the world to condemn the world; but that the world through him might be saved" (John 3:17, KJV). No matter who you are, where you are, or what you have done, God's love will reach you.

This Love Reconciles Us to God and Humankind

God's self-revelation in Christ is a personal message of love. More than angelic pronouncements or prophetic revelation, love came down clothed in the person of his Son. It was all the plan of God, initiated before the foundation of the world (1 Pet. 1:20). It is a love that, when accepted, precipitates reconciliation: we are reconciled to God and humankind. "All of this is from God, who reconciled us to himself through Christ and gave us the ministry of reconciliation" (2 Cor. 5:18).

No longer are we separated from God by a great gulf of rebellious independence. The cross of Christ has bridged the gulf. We who were once afar off have now been brought near by the Christ who courageously, yet compassionately, died for our sins. Reconciliation replaces alienation; we now experience the communion and companionship of the Father. God was never far from us—we were the ones wandering into a far country. Reconciliation does not change God; it changes us. God's love finds us where we are and brings us to where we should be with God.

Love's Reward: Immediate and Eternal

God's everlasting love assures us of his continuing beneficence. While his providential care reveals that the "rain falls on the just and the unjust," there are blessings assured those who live in covenant with God. Anyone who has experienced true love will acknowledge that while love does not remove us from the possibility of suffering, in love we lose sight of the suffering and sacrifice involved. Israel's retelling of their history in the Shema (Deut. 6:4-13) places the emphasis upon the blessings received from responding to the one true God. The early Christians emphasized the fact that the reward of God's love was always much greater than the persecution. James speaks of our reward: "Blessed is the man who perseveres under trial, because when he has stood the test, he will receive the crown of life that God has promised to those who love him" (1:12).

At no time does Scripture assure us that because God loves us with an everlasting love we will be exempted from trials and tribulations in this present world. The miracle of love is that when believers persevere, when they remain faithful in the midst of life's struggles, they will receive the reward that God has promised. It is to the loving children of the heavenly father that the Kingdom has been promised (James 2:5).

Jesus assures us that love's reward is both immediate and eternal (Mark 10:29-30). Our reward is not that which we take by violent overthrow of the material systems of this world, but it is the reward of the righteous, of those who obediently walk uprightly with the Prince of Peace. The meek shall inherit the earth. The poor in spirit will receive the Kingdom. And those who mourn will find comfort.

When your ego is devastated, your material wealth is depleted, and you deplore your situation in life, God's love does not leave you. By faith, accept it, and the reward becomes yours.

Love's Reciprocity

We love God because he first loved us. These words from 1 John remind us that our response is due to the fact that God expressed love to us through his Son, Jesus Christ. It is because of this that we respond, "Let us not love with words or tongue but with actions and in truth" (1 John 3:18). God's commandments are not grievous or burdensome to us; they become the delight of our life because they are carried out in love.

Such a love relationship is not weak, indulging one another in doing only what we like or enjoy. God's love is tough and tender. It is tender and sensitive to the total needs of the individual, redemptively reaching out to the whole person. But at the same time it is tough enough to say, "Those whom I love I rebuke and discipline" (Rev. 3:19). Through the events of life, many brought about by our personal decisions as well as circumstances, God is shaping our lives for his glory. Love responds to discipline positively. We learn from being tenderly rebuked because we know God first loved us.

> Savior, teach me, day by day,
>   Love's sweet lesson to obey:
> Sweeter lesson cannot be—
>   Loving him who first loved me.
>   —Jane E. Leeson

Hymnal of the Church of God, no. 414

Remember that in your relationship with God, you have this love in a very human vessel: "We have this treasure in jars of clay to show that this all-surpassing power is from God and not from us" (2 Cor. 4:7). The term *jars of clay* refers to a type of pottery that is easily broken. When God gave us his love, he was fully aware of our weakness. Therefore God assures us that the power to love comes from him. This does not imply that we are eternally secure, but it does assure us that we are eternally loved. Our security in Christ is conditioned on the basis of our responsive obedience to his will and the leadership of the Holy Spirit.

God's love makes you more than victorious. With Paul, you can say, "*I am convinced* that neither death nor life, neither angels nor demons, neither the present nor the future, nor any powers, neither height nor depth, nor anything else in all creation, will be able to separate us from the love of God that is in Christ Jesus our Lord."

Blessed Assurance
As Revealed in Scripture
Chapter 4
God's Love Is Everlasting!

Assurance That God First Loved Us
Isaiah 43:1, 4
This is what the Lord says—he who created you . . . he who formed you . . . "Fear not, for I have redeemed you; I have called you by name; you are mine. . . . Since you are precious and honored in my sight, and because I *love* you."
Jeremiah 31:3
The Lord appeared to us in the past, saying: "I have *loved* you with an everlasting love; I have drawn you with loving-kindness."

Hosea 11:4
I led them with cords of human kindness, with ties of *love*; I lifted the yoke from their neck and bent down to feed them.
1 John 4:19
We *love* because he first *loved* us.

Assurance That Love Is the Nature of God
1 John 4:7
Dear friends, let us *love* one another, for *love* comes from God. Everyone who *loves* has been born of God and knows God.
1 John 4:16
And so we know and rely on the *love* God has for us. God is *love*. Whoever lives in *love* lives in God, and God in him.

Assurance of God's Love Expressed in Christ
John 3:16
For God so *loved* the world that he gave his one and only Son, that whoever believes in him shall not perish but have eternal life.
Romans 5:8
But God demonstrates his own *love* for us in this: While we were still sinners, Christ died for us.
1 John 4:9-10
This is how God showed his *love* among us: He sent his one and only Son into the world that we might live through him. This is *love*: not that we loved God, but that he *loved* us and sent his Son as an atoning sacrifice for our sins.

Assurance That Love Motivates the Believer

2 Corinthians 5:14

For Christ's love compels us."

John 17:25-26

Righteous Father, though the world does not know you, I know you, and they know that you have sent me. I have made you known to them, and will continue to make you known in order that the *love* you have for me may be in them and that I myself may be in them.

Assurance That Love Disciplines

Revelation 3:19

Those whom I *love* I rebuke and discipline.

Assurance of Love's Effect

Proverbs 10:12

Hatred stirs up dissension, but *love* covers over all wrongs.

Assurance of Love's Endurance

Romans 8:38-39

I am convinced that neither death nor life, neither angels nor demons, neither the present nor the future, nor any powers, neither height nor depth, nor anything else in all creation, will be able to separate us from the *love of God* that is in Christ Jesus our Lord.

1 Corinthians 13:13

Now these three remain: faith, hope and *love*. But the greatest of these is *love*.

Chapter 5
There Is Power in the Blood!

For you know that it was not with perishable things such as silver or gold that you were redeemed from the empty way of life handed down to you from your forefathers, but with the precious blood of Christ, a lamb without blemish or defect.

—1 Peter 1:18-19

There Is a Fountain

There is a fountain filled with blood,
  Drawn from Immanuel's veins;
And sinners plunged beneath that flood,
  Lose all their guilty stains.
The dying thief rejoiced to see
  That fountain in his day;
And there may I, though vile as he,
  Wash all my sins away.
Dear dying Lamb, thy precious blood
  Shall never lose its power,
Till all the ransomed church of God
  Be saved to sin no more.
E'er since, by faith, I saw the stream
  Thy flowing wounds supply,
Redeeming love has been my theme,
  And shall be till I die.

                          —William Cowper

Hymnal of the Church of God, no. 347

How does one transmit Old Testament experience to a hi-tech, megatrend society? For those who work with computers, operate calculators and word processors, even visualize star wars, it is extremely difficult to communicate concepts that deal with tabernacles, priests, and sacrificial lambs. One even comes to the place of questioning whether this ancient teaching about the blood of Christ is necessary or helpful. And, as though we cannot be free of this ancient concept, in worship we have the audacity to sing:

> The blood that Jesus once shed for me
> as my Redeemer upon the tree;
> The blood that setteth the captive free,
> it will never lose its power.

Yes, no matter how sophisticated, educated, or theologically enlightened you may become, you can be sure that the blood that Jesus shed on the cross of Calvary will never lose its power.

The Bible Is Our Authority

Though divinely inspired, the Bible is not a book of science, but a book of faith. It reveals the mighty acts of God in history as he brought into being a people of his own. Each event from beginning to end carried with it significant symbolism to convey truth for all time. Ancient stories became the vehicles through which God's power was revealed and his purposes explained.

Life was recognized as a gift from God, a gift sustained by the blood that pulsated within (Lev. 17:11). And because of this life source, when one came to worship, sacrificial gifts were presented. These sacrifices were a symbol of the ultimate gift that one was capable of giving, the offering of life to the Giver of life. Sacrificial gifts were given as thank offerings and for forgiveness of sin. Blood was shed that a covering might be made for our failure (Gen. 3:21).

In the tabernacle and temple, ancient priests entered into the Holy of Holies where sin was forgiven by the sacrifice of the innocent for the guilty. Referred to in Hebrews, the writer speaks of the "blood of goats and bulls and the ashes of a heifer" being used to make us acceptable to God (9:13). More than through the power in this blood, the worshiper claimed God's forgiveness through faith and obedience. He knew that "without the shedding of blood there is no forgiveness" (Heb. 9:22). And thus we have this repetitive offering of sacrifices to find forgiveness, which fell far short of meeting the demands of a just and holy God. As repentant and obedient as the worshipers might have been, their offerings were ineffective in removing the guilt, shame, and condemnation that accompanied their sin. As Isaac Watts would write in his day,

Not all the blood of beasts
    On Jewish altars slain,
Could give the guilty conscience peace
    Or wash away the stain.

But even here is to be seen the blessed assurance that God is preparing a perfect sacrifice for our complete redemption. God gave positive assurance to his people when he said, "When I see the blood, I will pass over you" (Exod. 12:13). With his people in bondage and persecuted by the oppressor, God holds before them the promise of being saved by the blood of the Lamb. Once again it is portrayed in the writings of Isaiah as he speaks of the Suffering Servant: "Led like a lamb to the slaughter, and as a sheep before her shearers is silent, so he did not open his mouth" (53:7), or that one who trod the winepress alone and came forth from Bozrah "with his garments stained crimson" (63:1). God, with divine assurance, was preparing an everlasting sacrifice that would replace all the ancient traditions, making possible our complete redemption.

Christ Is Our Sacrifice

Truth in the Old Testament concealed is in the New Testament revealed. This everlasting sacrifice written of in the Old Testament now comes into fulfillment in the New Testament. John, beholding Jesus, exclaimed, "Look! the Lamb of God, who takes away the sin of the world" (John 1:29).

Beyond the virgin birth and the angelic annunciations, John saw more than the compassionate, miracle working Christ—he beheld the Savior of the world. Here was the Calvary Christ who would give his life a ransom for many. Angels had said he would "save his people from their sins" and Christ himself would declare that the Son of Man came to "seek and to save the lost" (Luke 19:10). To fulfill such a mission, it was necessary that, with a humble and contrite spirit, this Christ would lay aside his glory and become "obedient unto death—even death on a cross" (Phil. 2:8).

Prompted by divine love, Scripture says that "God demonstrated his own love for us in this: While we were still sinners, Christ died for us" (Rom. 5:8).

You cannot figure it out rationally. There is really little need for you to attempt to psychologize or demythologize the teaching of the sacrificial atonement of Christ. You will find no scientific explanation that will satisfy your quest. Christ's sacrifice is like a mother dying for a child she loves or a father perishing that a son might survive. Gradually you can begin to capture the picture of one who cares enough to give the ultimate, his very life's blood, in order that you might live. But this "blood" that was shed on Calvary is much more than that of martyrs, idealists, or lovers—it is God's divine gift of himself through the Son.

70

Writing about this Christ who gave his blood to redeem us, Herschel Hobbs said,

Not by His sinless life, impeccable in time and eternity, did Jesus redeem us. Not by His wondrous works, miraculously defying nature's course, did He redeem us. Not by His teachings, as *never man* taught, did he redeem us. Not by His preaching, as never man spake, did He redeem us. Not by His example, perfect with respect to God's law and beyond the reach of man's imitation, did He redeem us. Only by shedding His blood as the sacrifice for sinners, did He redeem us from sin and shame.[1]

Purchased by a Lamb without Blemish or Defect

In an affluent culture where materialism becomes the shrine of many, we must emphasize that the blood of Jesus paid for our transgressions. To "gain the world" only by popularity, prestige, and buying power leaves one poor, wretched, naked, and blind without the precious blood of the Lamb of God.

Sacrificial lambs had to meet particular requirements. They could not be sickly or have any defects. Special care was taken to make certain that the lamb was acceptable. Peter emphasizes this for us: "You know that it was not with perishable things such as silver or gold that you were redeemed from the empty way of life handed down to you from your forefathers, but with the precious blood of Christ, a lamb without blemish or defect" (1 Pet. 1:18-19). Christ alone could meet the re-

71

quirements. He was tempted in all points as we are tempted, yet without sin. He was reviled, but reviled not again. Christ and Christ alone is our sacrificial Lamb.

Cleansing through the Blood

You can be sure that there is no remedy for sin but the blood of Christ. It will never lose its power to save to the uttermost. Scripture and historical experience have taught us that you cannot be saved by joining the church, quoting the Bible, or living a good moral life. All of these fall short of redemption which can only be experienced through the power of the blood. It is the blood that brings forgiveness, enabling us to walk in the light as he is in the light (1 John 1:7). This divine grace has justified us from sin (Rom. 5:9) and has given us peace through his blood (Col. 1:20). But Jesus suffered outside the city gate to make the people holy through his own blood (Heb. 13:12). His blood not only justifies but also sanctifies. A. W. Tozer wrote,

I still believe in the power of the blood of the slain Lamb. And I still believe in its power . . . not only to protect . . . but to cleanse. You ask, 'How can it be?' and I must answer, 'I know not how it can be. How can it be that you can draw oxygen into your lungs by breathing, and the oxygen goes down into your lungs and is absorbed into the bloodstream to purify and give life?' Certainly I am not going to stop breathing because I cannot explain the mystery of how oxygen nourishes my life. Neither will I turn away from faith in this paschal Lamb. God cannot break his word—and no other lamb needs now to be slain.[2]

Yes, you can be sure that the blood will never lose its power. Through the blood you can be triumphant over sin and temptation because you have access to God and all the resources of heaven. Jesus, the Lamb of God, has paid the price for your full redemption. Claim by faith these words of William Cowper:

> Dear dying Lamb, Thy precious blood
> Shall never lose its power,
> Till all the ransomed church of God
> Be saved, to sin no more.

Footnotes

1. Hershel H. Hobbs, *Cowards or Conquerors* (Philadelphia: The Judson Press, 1951), p. 56.

2. *The Tozer Pulpit*, vol. 1 (Harrisburg, Pa.: Christian Publications, Inc., 1967), p. 125.

Blessed Assurance
As Revealed in Scripture
Chapter 5
There Is Power in the Blood!

Forgiveness through the Blood
Hebrews 9:22
In fact, the law requires that nearly everything be cleansed with blood, and without the shedding of blood there is no forgiveness.
Matthew 26:28
This is my blood of the covenant, which is poured out for many for the forgiveness of sins.

Cleansing through the Blood
Hebrews 9:13-14
The blood of goats and bulls and the ashes of a heifer sprinkled on those who are ceremonially unclean sanctify them so that they are outwardly clean. How much more, then, will the blood of Christ, who through the eternal Spirit offered himself unblemished to God, cleanse our consciences from acts that lead to death, so that we may serve the living God!
1 John 1:7, 9
If we walk in the light, as he is in the light, we have fellowship with one another, and the blood of Jesus, his Son, purifies us from every sin. . . . If we confess our sins, he is faithful and just and will forgive us our sins and purify us from all unrighteousness.

Redemption through the Blood
Romans 3:25
God presented him as a sacrifice of atonement, through faith in his blood. He did this to demonstrate his justice.
Ephesians 1:7
In him we have redemption through his blood, the forgiveness of sins, in accordance with the riches of God's grace.
1 Peter 1:18-19
For you know that it was not with perishable things such as silver or gold that you were redeemed from the empty way of life handed down to you from your forefathers, but with the precious blood of Christ, a lamb without blemish or defect.

Justification through the Blood
Exodus 12:13
The blood will be a sign for you on the houses where you are; and when I see the blood, I will pass over you.
Romans 5:9
Since we have now been justified by his blood, how much more shall we be saved from God's wrath through him!

Peace through the Blood
Colossians 1:20
And through him to reconcile to himself all things; whether things on earth or things in heaven, by making peace through his blood, shed on the cross.

Access to God through the Blood
Ephesians 2:13
But now in Christ Jesus you who once were far away have been brought near through the blood of Christ.
Hebrews 10:19-22
Therefore, brothers, since we have confidence to enter the Most Holy Place by the blood of Jesus. . . let us draw near to God.

Overcome by the Blood
Revelation 12:11
They overcame him by the blood of the Lamb and by the word of their testimony; and they did not love their lives so much as to shrink from death.

Chapter 6
Forgiveness Is Forever!

If we confess our sins, he is faithful and just and will forgive us our sins and purify us from all unrighteousness.

—1 John 1:9

Lord, Take the First Place

I yield to thee, Savior, forsaking my all,
  From sinful things now I will part,
To thee I surrender, for mercy I call,
  Come, take the first place in my heart.

O come, gentle Spirit, don't leave me, I pray,
  From thee I will never depart;
I come to thee now, for I cannot delay,
  Lord, take the first place in my heart.

I cannot be lost, Lord, for thee I will live,
  Forgiveness, O Savior, impart;
If I will confess thou wilt freely forgive,
  And take the first place in my heart.

The joybells of heaven will ring in my soul,
  My Savior, Redeemer, thou art;
To thee I surrender, wilt thou make me whole?
  Take now the first place in my heart.
                              —**Barney E. Warren**

Hymnal of the Church of God, no. 200

oes it sound too good to be true—this assurance by Scripture that when God forgives you it is forever? It is true! You can know that whatever sins have haunted you, hindering your whole-hearted commitment to Christ, or whatever failures have followed you, these can all be cast into the sea of God's forgetfulness to be remembered against you no more. (See Jeremiah 31:34.)

No doubt it is because of this universal need for forgiveness that one of the favorite stories in the Bible is found in Luke 15:11-24. It is often incorrectly referred to as the story of the bad boy who got into bad company, took up bad habits, and came to a bad end. We need to know that this is bad Bible interpretation.

The story, as we are reminded by Helmut Thielicke, the great German scholar/preacher, is that of a waiting, forgiving father. Capturing our attention because of its humanness, the story is that of a boy taking what the father gives him, and wasting it in worldy indulgences, only to come to an awareness that he has lost everything. In the agony of his guilt, he willfully makes the decision to return to his father and honestly confess his failure. But for me the beauty of the story is in the verse that reveals the boy on his way back home. "While he was still a long way off, *his father saw him* and was filled with compassion for him; he ran to his son, threw his arms around him and kissed him" (v. 20).

What a picture of acceptance and forgiveness! Have you ever wondered why it was that the father saw the boy when he was yet a long way off? Could it not be that while the boy had been gone the father kept on believing, expecting him to return home even when the family and everyone else gave up? Could it be a revelation of love unending, a love that never changed regardless of how far the boy may have gone or what he might have been accused of doing?

The father really loved the boy and each day watched expectantly, believing that the boy would return. Now he was back and the father immediately forgave him completely. No questions asked! No probationary period negotiated! It was forgiveness without limits. Forgiveness forever! Not once did the father heap guilt on him by reminding him that had he remained at home this would not have happened. He didn't even ask him what he had done with all the money. The father accepted the boy just as he was, believing in him, and in love forgave him forever.

The father's words indicate no thought of ever recalling this ordeal again. They indicate complete and irrevocable forgiveness as he says, Put the *best robe* on him. Put a *ring* on his finger. Put *sandals* on his feet. Let us celebrate forgiveness! Each act carries the symbolic meaning of permanence, that which is lasting, forever, never to be remembered by the father against the son.

Forgiveness Is for You

One of life's deceptions is the attitude referred to in First John of people who say they have never sinned. It is the unwillingness on our parts to acknowledge that we have failed, failed in being what God expects us to be. On my desk is a quotation, the kind you never want to forget, so you tape it to your desk to read each day. It reads, "Success is not final and failure is never fatal." Failure to do God's will is fatal only when we fail to seek his forgiveness. The Scripture says, "If we confess our sins, he is faithful and just and will forgive our sins and purify us from all unrighteousness" (1 John 1:9).

Sin is failure, missing the mark (*hamartia*). It is that failure on our parts to bring glory to God. "For all have sinned and fall short of the glory of God" (Rom. 3:23). Even those who have come to know Christ may fail to be faithful and return to the world from which they have been saved. (See 2 Timothy 4:10.) At the moment of yielding to temptation, falling into sin,

83

or backsliding, there is no more miserable feeling than that of failure. Guilt and condemnation engulf us. One reason we suffer such guilt is that we are without excuse. Sin is that which we willfully/knowingly commit or omit; it involves an act of the will on our parts. James clearly explains this for us as he outlines the progression from desire that entices us, to yielding that separates us from God, to death that destroys us. (See 1:14-15.)

Forgiveness in this context means *to leave behind*; literally, it means *to abandon* the sin, guilt, and condemnation that weigh down your life. Such forgiveness is appropriated by confession, that opening of your heart to God, exposing your being and behavior, becoming vulnerable in the ultimate sense. He alone is fully able to understand and to relate to this need. The writer of Hebrews declares, "For we do not have a high priest who is unable to sympathize with our weaknesses, but we have one who has been tempted in every way, just as we are—yet was without sin" (4:15).

To openly confess to Christ is cathartic, helping to bring healing and wholeness to your spiritual, physical, and emotional well-being. It allows all the hidden anger, resentment, guilt, condemnation, and all the sordid, sorry details of life to surface into the pure light of God's love. James even advocates that we would be healthier if we could come to the trust level within the family of God, to "confess [our] sins to each other and pray for each other," thereby finding healing and wholeness (James 5:16). Confession by a humble and contrite spirit brings about repentance, turning from the sin that has caused failure.

After Forgiveness, What?

Honest confession on the part of the sinner brings God's forgiveness, but the one forgiven must *accept what God has done* through Christ. Sometimes forgiveness is more than we can believe. The slow stain of sin has seeped so deeply into the soul that we are unable to believe that even God could forgive. But, upon the authority of his Word, God can, does, and will forgive if we will accept it by faith.

After accepting God's forgiveness, it then becomes necessary many times for us to *forgive ourselves*. How deeply we have hurt others, the manner in which we have failed our family or companion, and the reproach we have brought on the church seem unforgivable. Therefore, buried deep within are feelings of unworthiness and guilt that God has forgiven but with which we have failed to deal. God provides for us by making available to us an ally in the person of the Holy Spirit. Paul writes, "The Spirit helps us in our weakness. We do not know what we ought to pray, but the Spirit himself intercedes for us with groans that words cannot express. And he who searches our hearts knows the mind of the Spirit, because the Spirit intercedes for the saints in accordance with God's will" (Rom. 8:26-27).

Now we must *extend that forgiveness to others*. Within the gospel is a type of reciprocity: "Forgive us our debts, as we also have forgiven our debtors" (Matt. 6:12). And in Luke 6:37 we find, "Forgive, and you will be forgiven." That which has brought healing to us personally will also help relationally as we begin to apply this to our Christian faith. Forgiveness is forever, even when applied to those who may have wronged us. We need to forget the past as we have forgiven. It builds trust and acceptance, thus allowing for healthy harmony within the body of Christ.

I have blessed assurance that Jesus is mine, and as my Savior he forgives all my sin. You can be sure of this, too, because it comes from God, was purchased by the blood of Christ, and is administered each day by the Holy Spirit. Make this old song the testimony of your life this very moment as you claim his promised forgiveness.

I cannot be lost, Lord, for thee I will love,
    Forgiveness, O Savior, impart;
If I will confess thou wilt freely forgive,
    And take the first place in my heart.
                    —Barney E. Warren

Hymnal of the Church of God, no. 200

Blessed Assurance
As Revealed in Scripture
Chapter 6
Forgiveness Is Forever!

Forgiveness Promised
Jeremiah 31:34
For I will forgive their wickedness and will remember their sins no more.
1 John 1:9
If we confess our sins, he is faithful and just and will forgive us our sins and purify us from all unrighteousness.
2 Chronicles 7:14
If my people, who are called by my name, will humble themselves and pray and seek my face and turn from their wicked ways, then will I hear from heaven and will forgive their sin and will heal their land.

Forgiveness Is in Christ
Acts 5:31
God exalted him [Christ] to his own right hand as Prince and Savior that he might give repentance and forgiveness of sins to Israel.
Acts 13:38
Therefore, my brothers, I want you to know that through Jesus the forgiveness of sins is proclaimed to you.
Luke 23:34
Jesus said, "Father, forgive them, for they do not know what they are doing."

Forgiveness Is through the Blood
Ephesians 1:7-8
In him we have redemption through his blood, the forgiveness of sins, in accordance with the riches of God's grace that he lavished on us with all wisdom and understanding.
Colossians 1:14
In whom we have redemption, the forgiveness of sins.
Colossians 2:13-14
He forgave us all our sins, having canceled the written code, with its regulations, that was against us and that stood opposed to us; he took it away, nailing it to the cross.

Forgiveness of Others Required
Luke 6:37
Forgive, and you will be forgiven.
Mark 11:25
And when you stand praying, if you hold anything against anyone, forgive him, so that your Father in heaven may forgive you your sins.
Ephesians 4:32
Be kind and compassionate to one another, forgiving each other, just as in Christ God forgave you.

Chapter 7

All Things Are Possible!

I tell you the truth, anyone who has faith in me will do what I have been doing. He will do even greater things than these, because I am going to the Father. And I will do whatever you ask in my name, so that the Son may bring glory to the Father. You may ask me for anything in my name, and I will do it.

—John 14:12-14

By Thy Blessed Word Obeying

By thy blessed word obeying,
  Lord, we prove our love sincere;
For we hear thee gently saying,
  "Love will do as well as hear."
Every precept thou hast spoken
  Is essential to our life;
All thy mandates love betoken,
  To oppose them is but strife.
In thy wisdom, Lord, confiding
  We will follow in thy way;
With thy love in us abiding
  "Tis delightful to obey.
Each commandment thou hast given
  Is a waymark on the road
Leading up from earth to heaven
  To the blessed throne of God.
            —Daniel S. Warner

Hymnal of the Church of God, no. 252

Upon the authority of God's Word, we have the blessed assurance that all things are possible. Long before there was ever a Norman Vincent Peale on the East Coast or a Robert Schuller on the West Coast, the God of the Bible proclaimed that all things are possible. To demonstrate this possibility, God took a nondescript band of Arameans (Deut. 26:5) who were nobodies and made them into somebodies. Then, when the Flood came and everyone else perished, God made possible an ark in which Noah and his family were preserved. In the book of 2 Kings, chapter 4, when the widow was faced with eviction and her sons with slavery, God made possible a supply of oil with which she paid her debts. And you will recall how God delivered his people from Egyptian bondage, and made it possible for Joseph to survive in Potiphar's court, Daniel to sleep in the lion's den, and the three Hebrew children to walk in the fiery furnace.

How challenging to an age of science that demands a full, rational explanation of everything when all of the time our God transforms the impossible into the possible, truly making us realize that the wisdom of man is the foolishness of God. Whatever it is that seems impossible to you, Jesus says, "All things are possible to them that believe."

Possible to Become

God believes in you more than you believe in yourself. More than that, God has entrusted you with a priceless treasure: your own life. It is yours and you are responsible for what you do with it. Like all others you will be influenced by the home and community in which you live. Some of us will be poor; others rich. Some will be healthy and attractive; others very common and physically limited. We all discover sooner or later that life is not equitable: we are not all born with equal status and there are some great inequities in daily living. But these external influences need not determine what you do with this priceless treasure that God has given you—your life.

A severely handicapped young man commented that in the first twenty-one years of his life his mother taught him one great truth: "Never accept the limitations which other people impose on your life." These are the persons who, with supposedly good intentions, comment, "You're too slow to do that" or "You don't have

94

enough education to serve in that field." And even sometimes they say, "You're not attractive enough" or "You're too overweight to be an athlete."

How limited Jesus would have been in his ministry had he accepted the restrictions imposed on him by others. "Is not this the carpenter's son?" they asked. The implication was that you can't expect too much from one who came out of a carpenter's shop in the city of Nazareth. Poor economic status and bad community connections left him with very little possibility of ever breaking free from these severe limitations. But the truth of the matter is that this lowly Galilean accomplished the impossible. Recruiting a band of poorly educated fishermen, Christ helped to release in them their potential of becoming all they were meant to be. By personal invitation he called them to follow him, promising that if they would do so, he would make them become fishers of men. These disciples became the agents of change in the world as they discovered that all things are possible in Christ.

It is in this setting that one best understands the words in John 1:12: "To all who received him, to those who believed in his name, he gave the right to become children of God." This is the beginning point! It is possible for you to become a child of God. What tremendous implications this has for your life. It is the open door to success, victory, and triumph! Upon accepting Christ you immediately have available to you all the resources of heaven. Paul states it by writing, "All things are yours." You are under a divine guidance system, wherein the God of history volunteers to direct your life as you submit yourself to his will. As the Scripture says, "Trust in the Lord with all your heart and lean not on your own understanding; in all your ways acknowledge him, and he will make your paths straight" (Prov. 3:5-6).

Included in this is the power to follow obediently all that God leads you to do. He has provided more power than you will ever need to accomplish all that he has planned for your life. Jesus clearly states that all "authority in heaven and on earth has been given to [him]" (Matt. 28:18). And it is to those who dare to trust him that he has given the promise, "You will receive power when the Holy Spirit comes on you" (Acts 1:8). Here is what you have been looking for in your life: the possibility to become and the power to see it through. Are you hesitant about exercising this possibility? You can be sure it is true by taking God at his word and experiencing it personally in your life.

Possible to Believe

An early missionary is reported to have kept above his work space a plaque that read, "Attempt great things for God, expect great things from God." Sometimes we want to believe that all things are possible but we hesitate to attempt great things because we really don't expect them to happen. Is anything too hard for God? No, we believe that God can do anything but like the father in Mark's Gospel, we need some help in the area of our unbelief.

Especially is this true at a time when great

emphasis is being placed upon signs, wonders, and miracles. It is regrettable that in some areas of church life we judge spiritual success not by our faithfulness to God but by the magical, mystical events that take place in any given service. Such is not an acceptable biblical criterion for spirituality or faith.

All of the miracles recorded from the life of our Lord were only incidental to the real purpose of his ministry. Turning water into wine, healing the sick, and even raising the dead were side issues. Jesus came to save the world from sin. Therefore we read, "Anyone who has faith in me will do what I have been doing . . . even greater things than these, because I am going to the Father" (John 14:12-14). The great things referred to extend beyond these happenings. Jesus was pointing people to the Father. Signs and wonders were immediate but temporary. The presence of the Father would abide with them throughout all of life.

Yes, I do believe in miracles. To witness the touch of God through the prayer of faith, bringing healing to a fever-ridden body—these are miracles. But not nearly so great as when one whose life is fever ridden with sin becomes a new person in Christ through the prayer of faith. To see a financially bankrupt business prayed for and then succeed in the business world—that's a miracle. But it fades into nothingness when compared to a morally bankrupt life that is prayed for and is redeemed to the glory of God. All things are possible, and it is possible for you to believe if you will exercise the faith that God has entrusted to you. Faith the size of a mustard seed can so revolutionize your life you will experience miracles in your daily walk with God. One writer has said, "Faith is believing that it is so, even though it does not appear so, in order that it might be so, because it is so." Trust God today!

Possible to Be Positive

Believers in Christ are positive in their faith. Negative thinking is contrary to God's plan for your life. Like that great host of witnesses by which we are surrounded (Heb. 12:1), the Christian discovers that little is much when God is in it and that it is possible to be content in whatever state we may find ourselves (Phil. 4:11).

At the same time the believer discovers that we can do "all things" through this Christ who strengthens us and that we are free to ask "largely" of God those things that are in accordance with his will. Littleness of faith limits us in accomplishing the work of God. This does not mean that we attempt the bizzare, or over-extend ourselves foolishly, justifying the act by blaming God. Faith, that belief in the supernatural, is the belief that beyond what we are able to do in our own human strength and intellect, God can bring it to pass. Positively we affirm that God does give solutions to problems for which we have no answers. He is the divine source for our needs whether they be financial, physical, or relational.

God wants only your highest good. His steadfast love and grace witness to the positive nature of his plan for your life. As a young minister I heard the late G. Ray Jordan preach.

His eloquence and oratorical ability made me feel inadequate, almost defeated. He was professor of preaching at Candler School of Theology, Emory University in Atlanta, Georgia. But in that very meeting, Dr. Jordan introduced us to his book *You . . . Can Preach!* It was a positive declaration that when God has called us, he will enable us to succeed for his glory. Such is not success in the eyes of the world but in the kingdom of God where eternal standards of greatness matter most.

You can be sure that in your life all things are possible as you walk with the Lord. He is able to do "exceeding abundantly" above all that you ask or think. Paul said, "The one who calls you is faithful and he will do it" (1 Thess. 5:24).

Blessed Assurance
As Revealed in Scripture
Chapter 7
All Things Are Possible!

Possibilities through God
Genesis 18:14
Is anything too hard for the Lord?
Jeremiah 32:17
Ah, Sovereign Lord, you have made the heavens and the earth by your great power and outstretched arm. Nothing is too hard for you.
2 Samuel 22:29-34
You are my lamp, O Lord; the Lord turns my darkness into light. With your help I can ad-

vance against a troop; with my God I can scale
a wall. As for God, his way is perfect; the word
of the Lord is flawless. He is a shield for all
who take refuge in him. For who is God besides
the Lord? And who is the Rock except our
God? It is God who arms me with strength and
makes my way perfect. He makes my feet like
the feet of a deer; he enables me to stand on the
heights.

Psalm 37:4-6

Delight youself in the Lord and he will give
you the desires of your heart. Commit your way
to the Lord; trust in him and he will do this; He
will make your righteousness shine like the
dawn, the justice of your cause like the noonday.

Psalm 63:7-8

Because you are my help, I sing in the shadow
of your wings. I stay close to you; your right
hand upholds me.

Psalm 66:20

Praise be to God, who has not rejected my
prayer or withheld his love from me!

Psalm 145:13-14

The Lord is faithful to all his promises and
loving toward all he has made. The Lord upholds all those who fall and lifts up all who are
bowed down.

Possibilities through Christ

Matthew 19:26

Jesus looked at them and said, "With man this
is impossible, but with God all things are possible."

Matthew 28:18
Then Jesus came to them and said, "All authority in heaven and on earth has been given to me."
Philippians 4:13
I can do everything through him who gives me strength."

Possibilities through Faith
Matthew 21:22
If you believe, you will receive whatever you ask for in prayer.
Mark 9:23
Everything is possible for him who believes.
John 1:12
To all who received him, to those who believed in his name, he gave the right to become children of God.
1 John 5:4-5
This is the victory that has overcome the world, even our faith. Who is it that overcomes the world? Only he who believes that Jesus is the Son of God.

Possibilities through the Holy Spirit
Zechariah 4:6

"Not by might nor by power, but by my Spirit," says the Lord Almighty.
Acts 1:8
You will receive power when the Holy Spirit comes on you.

Chapter 8

There Is *Peace* Beyond Understanding!

Peace I leave with you; my peace I give you. I do not give to you as the world gives. Do not let your hearts be troubled and do not be afraid.

—**John 14:27**

Come, Holy Spirit, Still My Heart

Come, Holy Spirit! still my heart
 With gentleness divine;
Indwelling peace thou canst impart;
 Oh make that blessing mine!
Give me a heart of calm repose
 Amid the world's loud roar,
A life that like a river flows
 Along a peaceful shore!
Above these scenes of storm and strife
 There spreads a region fair;
Give me to live that higher life,
 And breathe that heavenly air.
Come, Holy Spirit! breathe that peace,
 That vict'ry make me win;
Then shall my soul her conflict cease,
 and find a heaven within.

Amen.

—Anonymous

Hymnal of the Church of God, no. 151

"**P**erfect submission, all is at rest" portrays a picture of peace and tranquility. The songwriter does not attempt to interpret the meaning for the worshiper. We are allowed the privilege of using our minds to visualize or imagine what it would be like to be at rest.

There really seem to be no words to help us adequately express or define what this peace is like; it is beyond understanding. One thing we do know: the Bible gives assurance that it is experienced by all who come to know the Prince of Peace, Jesus Christ. *Shalôm* in the Hebrew and *eirene* in the Greek carry the meaning of protection, preservation, and peace. It is the peace of God revealed in the person of his Son, Jesus Christ.

Peace is not necessarily the absence of struggle but the assurance that in the storms of life, God's steadfast love sustains us. No matter how severe the storm, Jesus never fails. I witnessed such peace in the life of a young family. Tragedy struck unexpectedly when the family's automobile was totally demolished in a highway accident. Five members of one family perished. Invited to participate in the memorial service, I traveled up into the North Carolina mountains to a small frame building which housed a Primitive Baptist Church. Nestled among the scrub pines, with a graveyard beside the building, the church building provided a sanctuary in the time of sorrow's storm.

As we shared together the Word of God, healing began to mend broken hearts. The choir sang softly:

Peace! Peace! wonderful peace,
Coming down from the Father above;
Sweep over my spirit forever, I pray,
In fathomless billows of love.

What strange alchemy was this, transforming tragedy into triumph, sorrow into song? No theologian could explain what happened as the peace of God settled down over the weeping congregation. No preacher with eloquent words could fully articulate the reality of peace experienced by those intimately related to the family. If you were to try to understand it psychologically it would only leave you grasping for words, words that always prove inadequate to define this peace that is beyond human understanding.

It Is the Peace That
Only Jesus Gives

Promised of God in the Scriptures and pro-claimed by prophets, peace became the desire of all God's people. In worship they could repeat, "You will keep in perfect peace him whose mind is steadfast, because he trusts in you" (Isa. 26:3).

And from the day of Christ's birth until he ascended to the Father, he became the embodi-ment of peace. His earthly ministry was marked by bringing peace to disturbed minds, stilling the storms of sin that raged, and giving rest to those who were tormented by guilt. As the Son of Man he entered fully into the experiences of his disciples. Candidly he had told them that in the world they would have tribulation. He dared to let them know that some would be rejected because of their belief in him. So sensitive was this Christ to our human situation that when his friend Lazarus died, "Jesus wept." He knew and experienced the stress, anxieties, and con-flicts of our humanity. But in spite of the struggle, Jesus had no desire for his followers to be taken out of the real world in which they ministered: "My prayer is not that you take them out of the world but that you protect them from the evil one" (John 17:15).

As children of God we are all confronted by conflict. Following Christ does not exempt us from the strain and stress of our society. The beauty of our faith is that in the midst of the storm there is a Savior who stands and with authority cries above the howling winds of adversity, "Peace! Be still!" And once again, beyond human understanding, peace is experienced.

Having lived with the disciples and knowing the stress under which they carried on their ministry, Jesus sought to prepare them for his impending death on Calvary. Taking the initiative, as God always does, Jesus said, "My peace I give unto you." It was not the casual, temporary peace of the world, snatched as a tranquil moment in time. Nor was it a soothing word to make them feel good about his going from them. Here was peace from the Prince of Peace—peace that could not be legislated, purchased, or demanded. It was the permanent peace that the world could not give or ever take away. Not even the disciples could fully understand. They could only experience it as they lived out their lives for Him.

Alexander Maclaren, one of the truly great preachers of the late 1800s, experienced peace at a time of great theological turbulence. When the faith of others was being shaken, Maclaren stood steady in the midst of the spiritual storms. He said, "Liberalism, the impact of evolution, the rising tide of the critical approach to the Bible, the wrestling with the complexities of modern life as it related to the Christian faith . . . all of these washed across Maclaren's life with the effect of a wave upon a mighty granite boulder . . . he was unmoved in his conservative evangelical position."* With such assurance it is not surprising that above the place of his entombment is a cross on which one finds the words "In Christ, *in peace*, in hope." He had discovered peace the world could not give and could never take from him.

It Is Peace with God

Although we are assured that Christ makes this available, "there is no peace" until one gets right with God. All of our attempts to relieve guilt and condemnation fall short of the desired result. Confession may lift the burden for a while, but unless sin is forgiven and a right relationship restored, there will be no lasting peace. Too often, our lives are comparable to the surface of the ocean, tranquil in appearance. But beneath the waves there is a tossing turbulence due to sin that is yet unconfessed. Nothing is more stressful to the human body than a guilty conscience. It is not fear of judgment but the discontent of a life that is not in harmony with a holy God.

Our quest for peace can only be realized when we are willing to stop resisting the Holy Spirit and surrender our lives to God—willing to cease rebelling and in submission, obediently follow after him in faith. Only then can we say, "Therefore, since we have been justified through faith, *we have peace with God* through our Lord Jesus Christ" (Rom. 5:1). Such peace can be verified by testing it with the Bible: "Therefore, there is now no condemnation for those who are in Christ Jesus, because through Christ Jesus the law of life set me free from the law of sin and death (Rom. 8:1-2).

You Can Experience the Peace of God

What a blessed assurance it is when we as believers come to realize that the battle against sin is over and Christ has become our peace, giving us the victory. What a joy to know that without question we do not need to work our way to heaven, struggling to accomplish all the great things that others may have done. The peace of God has come and we have entered into a spiritual "rest" promised in Scripture (Hebrews 4:9).

Now, through the fruit of the Spirit, this peace of God becomes productive. "Love, joy, peace, patience, kindness, goodness, faithfulness, gentleness, and self-control" (Galatians 5:22) now become the norm. The believer is able to live at peace personally and relationally. Attitudes are different because there is no longer a need to fight or rebel. We are at peace within and without as we relate to those about us in the family, the church, and the world. Your thoughts are now controlled by the Holy Spirit, the words of your mouth in conversation seek to exalt the Lord, even your financial stewardship has become subject to the higher will of God because you have surrendered to his control.

This peace does not mean that you will be free from all concern about the relational and material life. Concern is a healthy part of responsible Christian living and should be included in the disciplined life. We are at peace with God, and with each other, and the Holy

Spirit brings sanity and serenity to our daily living.

Peace Is Also a Process

Included in Scripture is an awareness of faith that is instantaneous and progressive. We are saved instantaneously but now we must so live that we may gain the reward of the righteous. As a believer, I have entered into peace with God and experience daily the peace of God. Now, however, I am responsible to share this peace with others whom I meet along the way. According to Hebrews 12:14, the person who is at peace with God must "make every effort to live in peace with all men and to be holy; without holiness no one will see the Lord." Those at peace with God seek to live peaceably with others. Jesus said, "Blessed are the peacemakers" (Matt. 5:9).

There is a happiness in holiness that produces peaceful living that attracts others to this experience in Christ. You can be sure that even when you cannot comprehend it, peace communicates the Christian life in a language everyone understands.

Blessed Assurance
As Revealed in Scripture
Chapter 8
There Is *Peace*
Beyond Understanding!

Promised to God's People
Psalm 85:8
I will listen to what God the Lord will say; he promises peace to his people, his saints—but let them not return to folly.
Psalm 4:8
I will lie down and sleep in peace, for you alone, O Lord, make me dwell in safety.
Psalm 29:11
The Lord gives strength to his people; the Lord blesses his people with peace.
Isaiah 26:3
You will keep in perfect peace him whose mind is steadfast, because he trusts in you.
Isaiah 32:17
The fruit of righteousness will be peace; the effect of righteousness will be quietness and confidence forever.

Prophecy Proclaimed Peace
Isaiah 9:6-7
For to us a child is born, to us a son is given, and the government will be on his shoulders. And he will be called Wonderful Counselor, Mighty God, Everlasting Father, Prince of

Peace. Of the increase of his government and peace there will be no end.

Isaiah 52:7

How beautiful on the mountains are the feet of those who bring good news, who proclaim peace, who bring good tidings, who proclaim salvation, who say to Zion, "Your God reigns!"

Isaiah 53:5

But he was pierced for our transgressions, he was crushed for our iniquities, the punishment that brought us peace was upon him, and by his wounds we are healed.

Luke 1:79

To shine on those living in darkness and in the shadow of death, to guide our feet into the path of peace.

Possible through Christ

Luke 2:14

Glory to God in the highest, and on earth peace to men on whom his favor rests.

Luke 24:36

While they were still talking about this, Jesus himself stood among them and said to them, "Peace be with you."

John 14:27

Peace I leave with you; my peace I give you. I do not give to you as the world gives. Do not let your hearts be troubled and do not be afraid.

John 16:33

I have told you these things, so that in me you may have peace. In this world you will have trouble. But take heart! I have overcome the world.

Romans 5:1
Therefore, since we have been justified through faith, we have peace with God through our Lord Jesus Christ.

Philippians 4:7
And the peace of God, which transcends all understanding, will guard your hearts and your minds in Christ Jesus.

Produced by the Holy Spirit

Romans 8:6
The mind of sinful man is death, but the mind controlled by the Spirit is life and peace.

Romans 14:17-18
For the kingdom of God is not a matter of eating and drinking, but of righteousness, peace and joy in the Holy Spirit, because anyone who serves Christ in this way is pleasing to God and approved by men.

Galatians 5:22
The fruit of the Spirit is love, joy, peace, patience, kindness, goodness, faithfulness, gentleness and self-control.

Peace Preserves Unity

2 Corinthians 13:11
Aim for perfection, listen to my appeal, be of one mind, live in peace. And the God of love and peace will be with you.

Ephesians 4:3
Make every effort to keep the unity of the Spirit through the bond of peace.

Ephesians 2:14-18
For he himself is our peace, who has made the
two one and has destroyed the barrier, the
dividing wall of hostility, by abolishing in his
flesh the law with its commandments and regulations. His purpose was to create in himself
one new man out of the two, thus making
peace, and in this one body to reconcile both of
them to God through the cross, by which he
put to death their hostility. He came and
preached peace to you who were far away and
peace to those who were near. For through him
we both have access to the Father by one
Spirit.
Colossians 3:15
Let the peace of Christ rule in your hearts,
since as members of one body you were called
to peace. And be thankful.

Chapter 9

There Is Hope by the Holy Spirit!

May the God of hope fill you with great joy and peace as you trust in him, so that you may overflow with hope by the power of the Holy Spirit.

—Romans 15:13

We Have a Hope

Have we any hope within us of a life beyond
    the grave,
      In the fair and vernal lands?
Do we know that when our earthly house by
    death shall be dissolved
      We've a house not made with hands?

We have a hope within our souls,
    Brighter than the perfect day:
God has given us his Spirit,
    And we want the world to hear it.
All our doubts are passed away.

Blessed hope we have within us is an anchor to
    the soul,
      It is both steadfast and sure;
It is founded on the promises of Father's
    written word,
      And 'twill ever more endure.

Since we've walked the strait and narrow way
    our path has ever shone,
      Brighter, brighter, day by day;
Hope within our hearts assures us it is better
    farther on,
      It is brighter all the way.

Life will end in joyful singing, "I have fought a
   faithful fight,"
   Then we'll lay our armor down;
And our spirits freed from earthly ties shall
   take their happy flight
   To possess a starry crown.
                              —**William G. Schell**

———

Hymnal of the Church of God, no. 443

Hope, that ultimate trust in the goodness of God, can be yours! It is the Christian's desirable expectation and pleasurable anticipation. Mentioned some 140 times in the Bible, hope is a blessed assurance for the believer. God planned it, his Word reveals it, Christ provides it, and the Holy Spirit implements it in your personal life. Christ not only came to free us from sin but also to liberate us from the pessimism and negative thinking that accompany sin.

It is possible for hope to be positive or negative. When used of God it is the source of eternal strength. But when used by the enemy of our souls it can be the path to ruin, deceiving us by sin's allurement. It is hope that lures gamblers on, making them believe that eventually they will experience the big win. And thieves, hoping that they will not get caught, continue to take wrongfully from others. Such hope, tainted by the slow stain of sin, leaves a trail of tragedy wherever it goes.

But when hope is implemented in our lives by the Holy Spirit, it becomes the light that shines in the darkness of despair. It is the shout of victory when the battle seems almost lost. Hope is like a cool breeze in the desert, bringing promise of water for the weary traveler. Best understood, hope is that tireless trust in God that goes on believing when everything else has been stripped away.

Paul believed that there were three great lasting qualities in life: "faith, hope, and love." The greatest of these, he said, is love. While love is the greatest, we sometimes fail to take note of the progression indicated by this passage in 1 Corinthians 13. Faith is that by which we are saved through grace (Eph. 2:8-9). Love is the ultimate in Christian experience, the "most excellent way" (1 Cor. 12:31). But the continuum that holds faith and love together is the blessed hope of the believer. In a world that runs from reality and fantasizes about the future, we Christians should be able to give to all who ask a reason for the hope we have within (1 Peter 3:15).

Hope Thou in God

Leslie D. Weatherhead, pastor of City Temple in London, commented, "When the Psalmist wrote: 'Hope thou in God,' he gave the world the only ground for hope that exists."* It was this *hope* in God that kept Israel striving for the promises that the Lord had given them in

Covenant. They would allow nothing to rob them of their belief in the sovereign power and goodness of God. Because of this hope, Israel could continue. Regardless of Israel's backsliding and bickering, chronic complaints, and alliances with pagan forces, there was always a remnant that held on to hope in God. It was the blessed assurance that when they had placed their hope in God, they could always trust him. God's covenant continues, his love is everlasting, and his Word will endure forever.

Hope Is More Than Human

We are incapable of saving and sustaining ourselves. Created in the image of God, redeemed by the grace of God, we require that which is supernatural to sustain us. Initially we are convicted by the Holy Spirit. Then when we are saved by grace through faith and have decided to follow the Lord, we discover the need for hope that sustains us in Christ. It is a hope that claims what we have not seen. It is the awareness that we *have been* saved, we are *presently being* saved, and ultimately we *will be* saved. One is initial, the second is progressive, and the third is final.

Although we are saved and forgiven immediately through faith, we have not yet experienced the final reward of the righteous. The question is not How well did you begin the race? but Will you finish it? Hope enables us to reach for that which we have not yet seen, although we accept by faith. Paul wrote: "For in this hope we were saved. But hope that is seen is no hope at all. Who hopes for what he already has? But if we hope for what we do not yet have, we wait for it patiently" (Rom. 8:24-25).

The Holy Spirit has brought us to Christ and now we patiently wait for the fulfillment of the reward as we abide in him in hope. If the ultimate Christian experience were something we could humanly achieve, see, and touch, then there would be no need for God. It is because of this spiritual and eternal aspect of our being that hope is essential. As heirs of God, we have this "hope of eternal life" (Rom. 8:16; Titus 3:7).

Overflow with Hope

God never shortchanges his people but always gives in abundance. Jesus promised that those who would give should receive "good measure, pressed down, shaken together *and running over*" (Luke 6:38). The Christian who gives all to God should be able to live out of the overflow of blessings.

As heirs of God, we have come into all the resources of heaven and the Holy Spirit enables us to appropriate this hope. We still face temptations and struggle with sin, but when these times come, the Holy Spirit helps our very souls overflow with hope. Rather than being driven about by the storms of life—sickness, failure, adversity—we are secured by hope: "We have this hope as an anchor for the soul, firm and secure" (Heb. 6:19).

It is out of this overflow that you discover what is meant by "Christ in you, the hope of glory" (Col. 1:27). You are sustained not by human strength, or by human wisdom, but by

Christ. His living presence within brings the hope of glory that is otherwise impossible.

Hold on to Hope

Every child of God should live in anticipation of the fulfillment of God's promises. The existentialist laughs at the so-called pie-in-the-sky theology. With a desire to serve only the present world, such a person loses sight of what God has prepared for those who love him. The believer in Christ, however, has the best of both worlds. Whatever we presently face—sickness or health, failure or success, life or death—we are constantly supported by the hope that is ours by the Holy Spirit.

The believer's hope does not end with threescore years and ten. It reaches beyond this present world. Paul writes, "If only for this life we have hope in Christ, we are to be pitied more than all men" (1 Cor. 15:19). God has already given us the victory. Christ has conquered over death and because he lives, we shall live also. Did not Jesus say, "I am going there to prepare a place for you. And if I go and prepare a place for you, I will come back and take you to be with me" (John 14:2-3)? We have this hope because we have placed our trust in him.

Hope carries us through and beyond our human limitations to the abundance of God's provisions made for his children. As joint heirs with Christ, we have this hope of glory in life beyond the grave. True Christian hope is not vague, it is valid! Hope thou in God. Hold on to hope!

Blessed Assurance
As Revealed in Scripture
Chapter 9
There Is Hope by the Holy Spirit!

Hope Thou in God
Psalm 42:5-6
Why are you downcast, O my soul? Why so disturbed within me? Put your hope in God, for I will yet praise him, my Savior and my God.
Psalm 146:5
Blessed is he whose help is the God of Jacob, whose hope is in the Lord his God.
Psalm 39:7
But now, Lord, what do I look for? My hope is in you.
Jeremiah 31:17
"So there is hope for your future," declares the Lord.

Hope of Salvation
1 Thessalonians 5:8
But since we belong to the day, let us be self-controlled, putting on faith and love as a breastplate, and *the hope of salvation* as a helmet.
Ephesians 1:18
I pray also that the eyes of your heart may be enlightened in order that you may know *the hope to which he has called you*, the riches of his glorious inheritance in the saints.

Titus 3:7
So that, having been justified by his grace, we might become heirs having *the hope of eternal life*.

Hope through the Holy Spirit
Romans 5:5
And *hope* does not disappoint us, because God has poured out his love into our hearts *by the Holy Spirit*, whom he has given us.
Galatians 5:5
But by faith we eagerly await *through the Spirit* the righteousness for which we *hope*.
Romans 15:13
May the God of hope fill you with great joy and peace as you trust in him, so that you may overflow with *hope by the power of the Holy Spirit*.

Hope of Glory
Romans 5:1-2
Therefore, since we have been justified through faith, we have peace with God through our Lord Jesus Christ, through whom we have gained access by faith into this grace in which we now stand. And we rejoice in *the hope of the glory of God*.
Colossians 1:27
To them God has chosen to make known among the Gentiles the glorious riches of this mystery, which is Christ in you, *the hope of glory*.

Hope in Patience
Romans 8:23-25
Not only so, but we ourselves, who have the firstfruits of the Spirit, groan inwardly as we wait eagerly for our adoption as sons, the redemption of our bodies. For in this *hope* we were saved. But hope that is seen is no hope at all. Who hopes for what he already has? But if we hope for what we do not yet have, we wait patiently.

Hope Is Joyful
Romans 12:12
Be *joyful in hope*, patient in affliction, faithful in prayer.
Romans 15:13
May the God of hope fill you with all joy and peace as you trust in him, so that you may *overflow with hope* by the power of the Holy Spirit.

Hope Is an Anchor
Hebrews 6:18-19
God did this so that, by two unchangeable things in which it is impossible for God to lie, we who have fled to take hold of the hope offered to us may be greatly encouraged. We have this *hope as an anchor* for the soul, firm and secure.
Hebrews 10:23
Let us *hold unswervingly to the hope* we profess, for he who promised is faithful.

1 Peter 3:15
But in your hearts set apart Christ as Lord.
Always be prepared to give an answer to everyone who asks you to give the reason for the
hope that you have.
1 John 3:3
Everyone who has this hope in him purifies
himself, just as he is pure.

Hope in the Resurrection
Acts 23:6
Then Paul, knowing that some of them were
Sadducees and the others Pharisees, called out
in the Sanhedrin, "My brothers, I am a Pharisee, the son of a Pharisee. I stand on trial
because of my *hope in the resurrection* of the
dead."
1 Corinthians 15:19-20
If only for this life we have hope in Christ, we
are to be pitied more than all men. But Christ
has indeed been raised from the dead, the firstfruits of those who have fallen asleep.
1 Peter 1:3
Praise be to the God and Father of our Lord
Jesus Christ! In his great mercy he has given
us new birth into *a living hope* through the
resurrection of Jesus Christ from the dead.
1 Peter 1:21
Through him you believe in God, who raised
him from the dead and glorified him, and so
your faith and hope are in God.

Chapter 10

God's Grace Is Sufficient!

From the fullness of his grace we have all received one blessing after another. For the law was given through Moses; grace and truth came through Jesus Christ.

—John 1:16-17

Amazing Grace

Amazing grace! how sweet the sound,
  That saved a wretch like me!
I once was lost, but now am found,
  Was blind, but now I see.

'Twas grace that taught my heart to fear,
  And grace my fears relieved;
How precious did that grace appear
  The hour I first believed!

Through many dangers, toils and snares,
  I have already come;
'Tis grace hath brought me safe thus far;
  And grace will lead me home.

When we've been there ten thousand years,
  Bright shining as the sun,
We've no less days to sing God's praise
  Than when we first begun.

—John Newton

Hymnal of the Church of God, no. 303

Grace is the beauty of God's face—too beautiful to look upon but so attractive that we cannot turn away. It is that unutterable beauty that creates trust, confidence, and optimism in the heart of the believer. Such a confidence becomes a surety of *sufficiency*: "He is able to do *exceeding abundantly* above all that we ask or think, according to the power at work in us" (Eph. 3:20).

Do you have that blessed assurance? I mean the personal assurance that God's grace is sufficient for you? Most of us have encouraged others by saying, "God's grace is sufficient for you!" To envision what we believe God can do for others is not too hard, but we often have some difficulty in appropriating God's grace for ourselves. For that reason, let me encourage you to accept by faith the blessed assurance that God's grace is sufficient for your personal life.

Grace is the very nature of God. It is God's undeserved, unchanging, unrestricted, unmotivated love for us just as we are. Because of grace, God persistently initiates the action that results in our opportunity for betterment.

God elects to love us before we ever love him. Therefore, his grace reaches out to us in our sin, revealing our separation and alienation, seeking to reconcile us to God through the redemption of Calvary.

Grace is more than the essential attitude of God; it is the active involvement of divine self-giving love as expressed in Christ. (See John 1:14, 16-17.) It is in Christ that grace and truth are best understood.

This inexhaustible, all-sufficient Savior becomes the embodiment of *grace*. Only such self-giving love is able to save to the uttermost, to heal the untouchable leper, to forgive the prostitute and her customers, to bless those who persecute you.

Healing of body, mind, and spirit find their sufficiency only in this Christ. Blinded eyes were made to see, troubled minds were given peace, and guilty souls found wholeness through his great salvation.

Grace makes available to us all the resources of heaven. Needs can be supplied, dreams can become reality, confidence can be reborn, and victory over defeat experienced. Grace knows no limits but is sufficient for old and young, powerless and powerful, poor or rich, illiterate or intellectual—it is sufficient for you!

Grace Is Sufficient

Two great events are lifted up for us in the Gospel of John: one points to Mount Sinai and the other to Mount Calvary. One symbolizes the Law, the other grace. The intent is not to diminish in any way the importance of Moses and the Law. Jesus said that he came not to destroy the Law, but to give spiritual meaning to its intent. (See Matthew 5:17.)

The writer in John 1:16-27 is attempting to help us comprehend the sufficiency of God's grace. The Law, though serving as a moral guide, was insufficient. It was incapable of forgiving, changing, or redeeming one's life. At its best, the Law was a "school teacher" (Gal. 3:24) pointing to Christ and freedom—freedom from the legalism and Pharisaism that limit and restrict.

Here is the contrast with that which is all-sufficient, the grace of God that supersedes the Law. True, "We are not under the law, but under grace" (Rom. 6:15) and in this grace we have "all received one blessing after another."

This grace is greater than religious ritual, traditional teachings, or historical heritage. St. Augustine said, "Law detects, grace alone conquers sin." Grace is greater in that it gave birth to the Law, went beyond the Law, and goes before us into eternity. (See Romans 5:1-2.)

Sufficient for Our Sin

Sin alienates us from God. It is selfish rebellion against the known will of God or omission of that which we know should have been done. Rather than a specific act, sin is an attitude of the heart and soul. "All have sinned and fall short of the glory of God" (Rom. 3:23) is the inclusive statement of Scripture. And it is in this state of sinfulness that we come to realize more fully the sufficiency of God's grace.

Only when recognizing the enormity of abounding sinfulness can we truly appreciate grace: "Where sin increased, grace increased all the more (Rom. 5:20). That which goes beyond our sin is the grace of God expressed in the love of Christ as he died on Calvary: "The wages of sin is death, but the gift of God is eternal life in Christ Jesus our Lord" (Rom. 6:23).

The most difficult people to save are those who have never sensed their lostness. Abraham Lincoln wrote of his day, "Intoxicated with unbroken success, we have become too self-sufficient to feel the necessity of *redeeming and preserving grace*, too proud to pray to the God that made us." Human nature has not changed. But in spite of our sinful self-sufficiency, self-pride, and individualism God's grace reaches out to save us.

It is in accordance with the "riches of God's grace" (Eph. 1:7-8) that our heavenly Father reaches after us and redeems us. He does not do this by works of righteousness, or the letter of the Law, but by his grace. Paul writes, "For it is by grace you have been saved, through faith—and this is not from yourselves, it is the gift of God—not by works, so that no one can boast" (Eph. 2:8-9).

In an age of self-help and do-it-yourself we need to emphasize that there is absolutely nothing you can do to save yourself. Grace only is sufficient and that is by the sovereign will of God. His grace liberates the captive, lifts up the fallen, and gives hope to the hopeless.

Once in grace always in grace? This question needs to be faced as we consider the greatness of this salvation. Many people have been led to believe that when once you have believed on the Lord Jesus Christ, nothing you do can cause you to be separated from God.

Such erroneous teaching is referred to as "eternal security" or "once in grace always in grace." The inference is that once you have been saved you can never again be lost. An oft-quoted text to support this is found in John 10:27-28: "My sheep listen to my voice, I know them, and they follow me. I give them eternal life, and they shall never perish; no one can snatch them out of my hand."

It is true that there is security for the believer but it is *conditional eternal security*. God's grace is sufficient to save you and to sustain you if you meet the conditions of his Word. Note that the passage in John 10 refers to those who are *"my sheep"* (already converted, known by God) and *"they follow me"* (indicating obedience to God's will). Grace is greater than our sin and is sufficient to keep us eternally if we walk in the light as he is in the light, obeying his will.

Sufficient for Our Suffering

Grace never fails to be sufficient for the immediate need that confronts us. It is triumphantly adequate to deal with any situation, even a crisis. Only in such events do we discover our sense of need, a need that demands assistance outside of ourselves. The suffering may range from the emotional trauma of a child on drugs, to terminal illness, business bankruptcy, or lingering affliction that drains energy and financial resources. It is a crisis moment in which you feel that you have reached your extremity in personal suffering.

As you reach beyond yourself for spiritual help, sensing that no other person can help you, you may have recalled the disciplines of faith. *Bible reading* may have alleviated some of your anxiety as you experienced God's closeness in the Twenty-third Psalm or the Lord's Prayer. Then, in *prayer*, you sought the Lord's peace as you cast your cares upon him, knowing that he cares for you. No doubt you were even tempted to bargain with the Lord, assuring him that if he would relieve the suffering, you would be more faithful to him. But after repeatedly seeking for God's relief, you listen as he speaks to you and the plain answer is no!

Isn't that what happened to Paul? He carried in his physical body a "thorn" and in earnest prayer at least three times he had petitioned God to relieve him. And then the answer was no! But here is the blessed assurance that every sufferer wants to hear: "My *grace is sufficient* for you: for my power is made perfect in weakness" (2 Cor. 12:9).

There is no argument here: Paul has already surrendered himself to live for God. Claiming sufficient grace for the suffering, Paul comments, "Therefore I will boast all the more gladly about my weaknesses, so that Christ's power may rest on me.... For when I am weak, then I am strong" (2 Cor. 12:9-10).

Some of the most saintly persons I have known experience severe suffering. No, the suffering did not make them saints. It was the all-sufficient grace of God that sustained them, keeping them sweet, preserving them from bitterness and cynicism.

C. W. Naylor, beloved servant of the church, spent years in bed, unable to walk, but he had a song in his heart as he wrote: "Whether I live or die, Whether I wake or sleep, Whether upon the land or on the stormy deep; When 'tis serene and calm or when the wild winds blow, I shall not be afraid—I am the Lord's I know."*

No matter how excruciating the pain, Jesus shares it with you and his grace is sufficient. No matter how heavy the burden, Jesus provides sufficient strength to lift the load. And in your moment of crisis, when no one understands how very much you are hurting, you can be assured by Scripture that his grace is sufficient for your suffering.

Sufficient for Your Shattered Dreams

Each time I read the Bible it reminds me of the song "Impossible Dream." Perhaps you remember that the song came out of a drama that depicted a young woman whose life and dreams had been shattered. But then, someone encouraged her to dream again. Dare to dream the impossible dream, reach for the unreachable star.

Grace is like that, sufficient to sustain you when your dreams are shattered. Sufficient to strengthen you in picking up the pieces and helping you put them back together again. No, grace does not make it all new. The scars remain, even though they are not always seen by others. But in a world of brokenness, there is One who initiates active involvement in helping to rebuild your world because he loves you.

Scripture says, "Your old men shall dream dreams" (Acts 2:17) but there are many young people in their teens who have already had their dreams dashed to pieces. Sometimes it is a case of abusive parents or peer pressure. Or it can be a case of too much, too soon, and their world explodes. Only grace is sufficient to put it back together again.

Or think of the countless numbers of families shattered as the home disintegrates. What was to be a bit of heaven on earth has become a place of turmoil, fighting, and bitter words. Such an atmosphere becomes the breeding ground for discontent and unfaithfulness. Beyond the counselors' chambers and the legal courts there is sufficient grace if we will allow God to help us pick up the broken pieces.

Yes, older people can be shattered, too. I am referring to some who go to pieces when they do not make a fortune by the time they are fifty. Or the one who lost a companion and because of that sorrow allowed his or her world to crumble. And too many of us keep looking back, trying to imagine how much better it would have been had we done differently. In an attempt to regain some lost dream we destroy the wonderful life that is possible today.

Yes, you can have the blessed assurance that God's grace is sufficient for your shattered dreams. Even when it hurts so badly that you cannot talk about it, the Holy Spirit understands. Paul writes, "The Spirit helps in our weakness. We do not know what we ought to pray, but the Spirit himself *intercedes for us with groans that words cannot express* (Rom. 8:26).

Grace! What a beautiful word. We could not and cannot earn it. We do not merit it. Grace is that inexpressible, active love of God that sought us in sin, saved us by his blood, sustained us in our suffering, and is sufficient for helping us mend our shattered dreams and go on living.

Note

Hymnal of the Church of God, no. 429

Blessed Assurance
As Revealed in Scripture
Chapter 10
God's Grace Is Sufficient!

Grace Is God's Nature
Psalm 84:11
For the Lord God is a sun and shield: the Lord
will give *grace* and *glory*: no good thing will he
withhold from them that walk uprightly. (KJV)
Psalm 103:8
The Lord is compassionate and gracious, slow
to anger, abounding in love.

Grace and Humility
Proverbs 3:34
He mocks proud mockers but gives grace to the
humble.
James 4:6
But he gives us more grace. That is why Scripture says: "God opposes the proud but gives
grace to the humble."
1 Peter 5:5
Young men, in the same way be submissive to
those who are older. . . . Clothe yourselves with
humility toward one another, because, "God
opposes the proud but gives grace to the
humble."

Grace Incarnate in Christ
John 1:14
The Word became flesh and made his dwelling
among us. We have seen his glory, the glory of

the One and Only, who came from the Father, full of grace and truth.
John 1:16-17
From the fullness of his grace we have all received one blessing after another. For the law was given through Moses; grace and truth came through Jesus Christ.
2 Corinthians 8:9
For you know the grace of our Lord Jesus Christ, that though he was rich, yet for your sakes he became poor, so that you through his poverty might become rich.

Grace Given Freely to All
Romans 11:5-6
So, too, at the present time there is a remnant chosen by grace. And if by grace, then it is no longer by works; if it were, grace would no longer be grace.
Ephesians 1:5-6
In love he predestined us to be adopted as his sons through Jesus Christ, in accordance with his pleasure and will—to the praise of his glorious grace, which he has freely given us in the One he loves.

Grace Teaches Us
Titus 2:11
For the grace of God that brings salvation has appeared to all men.

Grace and Salvation

Romans 3:22-24

This righteousness from God comes through faith in Jesus Christ to all who believe. There is no difference, for all have sinned and fall short of the glory of God, and are justified freely by his grace through the redemption that came by Christ Jesus.

Romans 5:1-2

Therefore, since we have been justified through faith, we have peace with God through our Lord Jesus Christ, through whom we have gained access by faith into this grace in which we now stand. And we rejoice in the hope of the glory of God.

Romans 5:15

But the gift is not like the trespass. For if the many died by the trespass of the one man, how much more did God's grace and the gift that came by the grace of the one man, Jesus Christ, overflow to the many!

Romans 5:17

For if, by the trespass of the one man, death reigned through that one man, how much more will those who receive God's abundant provision of grace and of the gift of rightousness reign in life through the one man, Jesus Christ.

Romans 5:20-21

The law was added so that the trespass might increase. But where sin increased, grace increased all the more, so that, just as sin reigned in death, so also grace might reign through righteousness to bring eternal life through Jesus Christ our Lord.

Romans 6:14
For sin shall not be your master, because you
are not under law, but under grace.
Ephesians 1:7-8
In him we have redemption through his blood,
the forgiveness of sins, in accordance with the
riches of God's grace that he lavished on us
with all wisdom and understanding.
Ephesians 2:4-9
But because of his great love for us, God, who
is rich in mercy, made us alive with Christ even
when we were dead in transgressions—it is by
grace you have been saved. And God raised us
up with Christ and seated us with him in the
heavenly realms in Christ Jesus, in order that
in the coming ages he might show the incom-
parable riches of his grace, expressed in his
kindness to us in Christ Jesus. For it is by
grace you have been saved, through faith—and
this not from yourselves, it is the gift of God—
not by works, so that no one can boast.

Grace Proclaimed
Acts 14:3
So Paul and Barnabas spent considerable time
there, speaking boldly for the Lord, who confirmed the message of his grace by enabling
them to do miraculous signs and wonders.

Grace and Christian Growth
Acts 4:33
With great power the apostles continued to
testify to the resurrection of the Lord Jesus,
and much grace was upon them all.

2 Corinthians 4:15
All this is for your benefit, so that the grace
that is reaching more and more people may
cause thanksgiving to overflow to the glory of
God.
2 Peter 3:18
But grow in the grace and knowledge of our
Lord and Savior Jesus Christ. To him be glory
both now and forever! Amen.

Grace and Confidence
Colossians 4:6
Let your conversation be always full of grace,
seasoned with salt, so that you may know how
to answer everyone.
2 Thessalonians 2:16-17
May our Lord Jesus Christ himself and God
our Father, who loved us and by his grace gave
us eternal encouragement and good hope, encourage your hearts and strengthen you in
every good deed and word.
Hebrews 4:16
Let us then approach the throne of grace with
confidence, so that we may receive mercy and
find grace to help us in our time of need.

Grace Strengthens Us
2 Corinthians 12:9
But he said to me, "My grace is sufficient for
you, for my power is made perfect in weakness."
Therefore I will boast all the more gladly about
my weaknesses, so that Christ's power may
rest on me.

2 Timothy 2:1
You then, my son, be strong in the grace that is in Christ Jesus.
Hebrews 13:9
Do not be carried away by all kinds of strange teachings. It is good for our hearts to be strengthened by grace, not by ceremonial foods, which are of no value to those who eat them.

Chapter 11

The Kingdom Has Come!

Once, having been asked by the Pharisees when the kingdom of God would come, Jesus replied, "The kingdom of God does not come visibly, nor will people say, 'Here it is,' or 'There it is,' because the kingdom of God is within you."

—Luke 17:20-21

All Hail the Power of Jesus' Name

All hail the power of Jesus' name!
  Let angels prostrate fall;
Bring forth the royal diadem,
  And crown him Lord of all.

Ye chosen seed of Israel's race,
  Ye ransomed from the fall,
Hail him who saves you by his grace,
  And crown him Lord of all.

Let every kindred, every tribe,
  On this terrestrial ball,
To him all majesty ascribe,
  And crown him Lord of all.

O that, with yonder sacred throng,
  We at his feet may fall;
We'll join the everlasting song,
  And crown him Lord of all.
        —Edward Perronet

Hymnal of the Church of God, no. 66

Confusion is the enemy of certitude. Rather than stabilize our faith, it creates conflict in the mind of the believer, making it difficult to accept the assurance of God's Word. Confusion exists within the church world regarding the kingdom of God. It is because of this that I want to put in print the truth that *you can be sure that the kingdom of God has come.*

Some clarification is needed due to the diversity of doctrinal teachings on the subject of the kingdom and last things. Because of this diversity, some choose to ignore the subject altogether, while others are caught up in the vast array of films, seminars, and sermons. We associate certain words with this study of last things (eschatology). *Armageddon, millennium,* and *rapture* are all a part of this theological mix.

Caution in biblical interpretation should be exercised as you study the Bible on this subject. The word *rapture* is not to be found in Scripture; it is a term developed to support one of our many theories. A literal interpretation of *Armageddon* ignores the reality of the spiritual conflict in which the church at this very moment is involved. "We wrestle not against flesh and blood—but against principalities and powers—rulers of darkness" (Eph. 6:12).

The verse in Revelation 20 wherein the term *thousand (millennia)* is found is used figuratively, referring to a long period of time. In no way is it connected scripturally to a pre- or post-millennial teaching wherein Christ rules for a thousand years on this earth. Scripture says that when the Lord returns, "the dead in Christ will rise first. After that, we who are still alive and are left will be caught up *with them* in the clouds to meet the Lord in the air. And so we will be with the Lord forever" (1 Thess. 4:16-17). Placing that passage in context with 2 Peter 3:10 leaves no place or time for a millennial fulfillment.

What assurance does God give regarding the Kingdom?

God Does Have a Kingdom

You can be sure that the kingdom of God foretold in Scripture became a reality through Christ's life, death, and resurrection. Hebrew history reveals that the people of God have always dreamed of an earthly king and kingdom—a kingdom that would exalt their history and bring all their enemies into subjection to their rule. But God's kingdom exceeded their expectation. "The God of heaven will set up a kingdom that will never be destroyed. . . . it will itself endure forever" (Dan. 2:44). Such a kingdom was to transcend all divisions and discrimination, for it would comprise "all people, nations, and . . . every language" (Dan. 7:14) and the one desire of these people would be to serve God.

No, the dream of such a kingdom was not merely theoretical, it was theological. The Kingdom was a theology that became reality. To fulfill God's plan and purpose it was and is essential that the Kingdom be spiritual in nature. "God is Spirit, and his worshipers must worship in spirit and in truth" (John 4:24).

Jesus Is the King

"When the time had fully come" (Gal. 4:4) God sent forth his son, announced by angels (Luke 1:30-33), born of a virgin, and acknowledged by John the baptizer (Matt. 3:1-2; John 1:29). It was with certainty that Jesus said, "I am *the* way, *the* truth, and *the* life; no one comes to the Father but by me" (John 14:6). Jesus knew who he was and why he was here.

Jesus shattered all the human concepts of what a king should be. His mother was a peasant woman, not a woman of royalty. He was born in a stable, not in a palace. Economically he lived in poverty, never in wealth. His entry into Jerusalem was on a donkey, not on a stallion. He died on a cross, not in comfort. And he was buried in a borrowed tomb. But the world knew him for who he was. As he entered

Jerusalem people cried, "Blessed is the King" (Luke 19:38) and when he died, the inscription for all to read was, "This is the King of the Jews" (Luke 23:38). But more than that, Christ is the King of Kings for all people of all ages and he shall reign forever and ever (Rev. 19:16).

The Kingdom Has Come

It is hard to recognize or enter into that which has not come into being. For that very reason the Bible is clear in revealing that John announced the Kingdom, Jesus preached it, and people entered into it. Had it been some future millennial concept, it would have been difficult to enter (Luke 16:16) when proclaimed by Jesus.

The kingdom of God is spiritual, not literal. It is present, not future. John Bright, the noted scholar, writes that in "the Old Testament, God's kingdom was always a future, indeed an eschatological thing, and must always be spoken of in the future tense.... But in the New Testament we encounter a change: the tense is a resounding present indicative—*the Kingdom is here!*"*

Such a kingdom was located in the hearts of the people of God, his loyal subjects (Luke 17:20-21). These were persons who had been born again through repentance and lived under the sovereign rule of Christ. Christ was not waiting for some futuristic Kingdom; already he was reigning over the people of God.

God does not want you to wait for that which is already available to his children. The nature of his Kingdom, Paul writes, is "not a matter of eating and drinking, but of righteousness, *peace*, and *joy* in the Holy Spirit" (Rom. 14:17).

While some sing of peace in the valley eventually, it is possible for the lion to live peaceably with the lamb in this present world. When Christ rules as King, peace prevails. One need not dream of the desert blooming like a rose in the future; there is power available to make your barren life productive. And there is no need to fight, trying to usher in the Kingdom by the arm of flesh. The Kingdom has come and we need no longer struggle (John 18:36).

Subjects of the King

Jesus placed priority on being born again, before being able to see the Kingdom (John 3:3). Then he emphasized the fact that we should seek first the Kingdom (Matt. 6:33) and his righteousness. Entering the Kingdom is distinctly different from joining a lodge or a service club. It is much more than a political party or religious organization. Only through an experience of grace—spiritual rebirth—can one truly enter the kingdom of God. It was because of this that Paul said, "flesh and blood cannot inherit the Kingdom of God" (1 Cor. 15:50). Family connections will not suffice. It is necessary that one personally be born again to enter the Kingdom and receive its blessings.

Attached to "seeking the Kingdom" is the admonition to seek also "his righteousness." To acknowledge Christ as King is to carry out Christ's life-style and system of values. "Holiness unto the Lord" was the word of the Old Testament. In the New Testament the standard of behavior is determined by our belief in

153

the moral righteousness of our God. Though tempted in all points as we are tempted, Jesus triumphed over sin. Now by the power of the Holy Spirit our lives in the Kingdom are to be victorious over this present world.

Moral purity, ethical integrity, and theological sanity are basic Kingdom values. For when we seek the righteousness that brings true spiritual worship, continual social justice, and an increased sensitivity to God, we can be sure that "all these things" will be added unto us.

Christ's subjects know that Kingdom rule is *theocratic*, not democratic. In becoming part of the Kingdom you accept the truth that Christ always has the final word. A majority vote does not overrule the Word of God. Too often a well-meaning majority may well be wrong. In the Kingdom our human will must always be subject to the divine will. We are subjects of the King! What we interpret as the will of God must always be in accordance with the Word and the Spirit.

Servants of the King

Jesus understands our humanness. He knows of the legitimate ambitions and desires within each person. For that reason, Christ left us an example of how Kingdom people really live. Though equal with God, Jesus laid aside his glory and became a servant—and died for the sins of the world (Phil. 2:7-8). Here is true greatness in the Kingdom. Power is not in the position held but in the person who is humble and contrite in spirit. The disciples could hardly accept it when Jesus rose from the table, girded himself with a towel, and then with a basin of water began to wash their feet (John 13:4-5). His example was one of servanthood in the Kingdom.

True subjects of the King, born again in the nature of Christ, will always find their fulfillment in servanthood. Carnal, selfish ambition and pride have been surrendered to the higher will of God. No longer are we striving for the primary positions of authority in the Kingdom (Mark 10:35-40). In the Kingdom we are all servants—not presidents, dignitaries, chairpersons of boards or chief executive officers. Significant, lasting contribution is not measured by how much money you made, how long you were in office, or how many persons you managed, but by how much of a servant you were.

True greatness in the Kingdom of God is attributed only to those who humbly and faithfully serve as in Matthew 25:31-40. Now let us pray those words together: "Thy Kingdom come. Thy will be done—"

The Kingdom has come, but only you can be sure if you are serving the King of Kings.

Notes

*John Bright, *The Kingdom of God* (Nashville: Abingdon Press, 1953), p. 197.

Blessed Assurance
As Revealed in Scripture
Chapter 11
The Kingdom Has Come!

An Everlasting Kingdom Foretold
Daniel 2:44-45
In the time of those kings, the God of heaven will set up a kingdom that will never be destroyed, nor will it be left to another people. It will crush all those kingdoms and bring them to an end, but it will itself endure forever. This is the meaning of the vision of the rock cut out of a mountain, but not by human hands—a rock that broke the iron, the bronze, the clay, the silver and the gold to pieces.

Daniel 7:13-14, 27
In my vision at night I looked, and there before me was one like a son of man, coming with the clouds of heaven. He approached the Ancient of Days and was led into his presence. He was given authority, glory and sovereign power; all peoples, nations and men of every language worshiped him. His dominion is an everlasting dominion that will not pass away, and his kingdom is one that will never be destroyed.... Then the sovereignty, power and greatness of the kingdoms under the whole heaven will be handed over to the saints, the people of the Most High. His kingdom will be an everlasting kingdom, and all rulers will worship and obey him.

Kingdom Announced by John
Matthew 3:1-2
In those days John the Baptist came, preaching in the Desert of Judea and saying, "Repent, for the kingdom of heaven is near."

Jesus Acknowledged as King
Luke 1:30-33
But the angel said to her, "Do not be afraid, Mary, you have found favor with God. You will be with child and give birth to a son, and you are to give him the name Jesus. He will be great and will be called the Son of the Most High. The Lord God will give him the throne of his father David, and he will reign over the house of Jacob forever; his kingdom will never end."

Luke 19:38
Blessed is the king who comes in the name of the Lord! Peace in heaven and glory in the highest!

Luke 23:38
There was a written notice above him, which read: THIS IS THE KING OF THE JEWS.

1 Timothy 6:14-15
To keep this commandment without spot or blame until the appearing of our Lord Jesus Christ, which God will bring about in his own time—God, the blessed and only Ruler, the King of kings and Lord of lords.

Revelation 19:11-17
I saw heaven standing open and there before me was a white horse, whose rider is called Faithful and True. With justice he judges and

makes war. His eyes are like blazing fire, and on his head are many crowns. He has a name written on him that no one but he himself knows. He is dressed in a robe dipped in blood, and his name is the Word of God. The armies of heaven were following him, riding on white horses and dressed in fine linen, white and clean. Out of his mouth comes a sharp sword with which to strike down the nations. "He will rule them with an iron scepter." He treads the winepress of the fury of the wrath of God Almighty. On his robe and on his thigh he has this name written: KING OF KINGS AND LORD OF LORDS. And I saw an angel standing in the sun, who cried in a loud voice to all the birds flying in midair, "Come, gather together for the great supper of God."

Jesus Proclaimed the Kingdom
Matthew 4:23
Jesus went throughout Galilee, teaching in their synagogues, preaching the good news of the kingdom, and healing every disease and sickness among the people.
Mark 1:14-15
After John was put in prison, Jesus went into Galilee, proclaiming the good news of God. "The time has come," he said. "The kingdom of God is near. Repent and believe the good news!"
Mark 9:1
And he said to them, "I tell you the truth, some who are standing here will not taste death before they see the kingdom of God come with power."

Luke 12:31-32
But seek his kingdom, and these things will be given to you as well. Do not be afraid, little flock, for your Father has been pleased to give you the kingdom.

Luke 16:16
The Law and the Prophets were proclaimed until John. Since that time, the good news of the kingdom of God is being preached, and everyone is forcing his way into it.

Kingdom Declared To Be Spiritual

Luke 17:20-21
Once, having been asked by the Pharisees when the kingdom of God would come, Jesus replied, "The kingdom of God does not come visibly, nor will people say, 'Here it is,' or 'There it is,' because the kingdom of God is within you."

John 18:36
Jesus said, "My kingdom is not of this world. If it were, my servants would fight to prevent my arrest by the Jews. But now my kingdom is from another place."

Romans 14:17
For the kingdom of God is not a matter of eating and drinking, but of righteousness, peace and joy in the Holy Spirit.

Entrance into the Kingdom

Matthew 3:2
And saying, "Repent, for the kingdom of heaven is near."

Mark 10:13-15

People were bringing little children to Jesus to have him touch them, but the disciples rebuked them. When Jesus saw this, he was indignant. He said to them, "Let the little children come to me, and do not hinder them, for the kingdom of God belongs to such as these. I tell you the truth, anyone who will not receive the kingdom of God like a little child will never enter it."

Colossians 1:13

For he has rescued us from the dominion of darkness and brought us into the kingdom of the Son he loves.

Greatness in the Kingdom

Matthew 18:1-4

At that time the disciples came to Jesus and asked, "Who is the greatest in the kingdom of heaven?" He called a little child and had him stand among them. And he said: "I tell you the truth, unless you change and become like little children, you will never enter the kingdom of heaven. Therefore, whoever humbles himself like this child is the greatest in the kingdom of heaven.

Chapter 12

The Resurrection Is for Real!

Jesus said to her, "I am the resurrection and the life. He who believes in me will live, even though he dies; and whoever lives and believes in me will never die."

—John 11:25

Alleluia! Alleluia!

Alleluia! alleluia! Hearts to heaven and voices raise;
Sing to God a hymn of gladness, Sing to God
   a hymn of praise,
He who on the cross as Savior For the world's
   salvation bled,
Jesus Christ, the King of Glory, Now is risen
   from the dead.

Now the iron bars are broken, Christ from death
   to life is born,
Glorious life, and life immortal, On this holy
   Easter morn;
Christ has triumphed, and we conquer By his
   mighty enterprise,
We with him to life eternal By his
   resurrection rise.

Alleluia! alleluia! Glory be to God on high;
Alleluia to the Savior Who has won the victory;
Alleluia to the Spirit, Fount of love and sanctity;
Alleluia! Alleluia! To the Triune Majesty.

Amen.

—Christopher Wordsworth

Hymnal of the Church of God, no. 120

pen, honest, willful confession can be therapeutic. Healthy confession serves as a release for inner guilt, anxiety, or concern. It can be very positive.

Let me confess that this chapter is not easy for me to write. The reason? I have never as yet experienced that of which I write. It is all by faith and hope and the blessed assurance which we have in Christ. Yes, I have experienced the death of loved ones and by faith accept that which the Word of God assures us is the reward of the righteous. We live in that blessed hope but our humanness longs for the certainty of life beyond the grave.

I was encouraged to continue writing this chapter by reading the words of Walter Brueggemann in his book *The Bible Makes Sense*. "The central concerns of the Bible are not flat certitudes but assurances that are characterized by risk and open mystery. The quality of certitude offered by the Bible is never that of a correct answer but rather *a trusted memory, a dynamic message, a restless journey, a faithful voice.* Such assurances leave us restless and tentative in the relation, and always needing to decide afresh. Rather than closing out things in a settled resolution, they tend to open things out, always in fresh and deep question and urgent invitation. The central thrust of the Bible, then, is to raise new questions, to press exploration of new dimensions of fidelity, new spheres for trusting. Such questions serve as invitations to bolder, richer faithfulness."[1] This I have found to be true and believe that in our quest we shall discover that the Resurrection is for real.

A Trusted Memory

The New Testament writers clearly remembered the last events in the life of Christ; some of the writers were there when it happened. The crucifixion, death, and resurrection of Christ became the central theme of their message.

Though they did not comprehend, the writers did trust what they fully remembered. They remembered the rolling away of the stone from the tomb, the angelic beings announcing the Resurrection, and the Lord's appearance to Mary Magdalene. They remembered minute things like the grave clothes, or that Peter and the "other disciple" (John 20:2-4) raced to the tomb and the "other disciple" got there first.

They remembered that Christ's resurrection form was recognizable but different. He appeared to the disciples, then later he appeared to them again to help Thomas as he struggled with this miracle of God's power. To assure the disciples and bring them together, the Risen Lord ate breakfast with them at the seashore.

Still later, Paul said, Jesus appeared to some five hundred persons (1 Cor. 15:6). Truly, it was an unforgettable experience. Death was really defeated. Christ bodily rose from the dead. And forevermore this living Lord was turned loose on the world, assuring us that there is life after death. It was this fulfillment of his words to Mary and Martha, "I am the resurrection and the life." The words of the prophets and Moses had been fulfilled (Acts 26:22-23).

This was an assurance built upon a trusted memory, one that was remembered by persons who discovered the reality of the Resurrection. It is a memory in which you can place your trust and on which you can hold in the future.

A Dynamic Message

"Go quickly and tell" (Matthew 28:7) was the directive given to those who witnessed the Resurrection event. It was a joy that could not be contained. Here is the excitement of the Easter story: it is the bodily resurrection of Christ from the grave, an event that validates and authenticates all of his other claims. Because of his living and abiding presence, the disciples could now come from behind closed doors and share the Good News with others. "If Christ has not been raised, our preaching is useless" (1 Cor. 15:14) were Paul's words for consideration, but now they knew without doubt that he was alive. Therefore, the message became the focal point for New Testament preaching and teaching.

Peter's powerful Pentecostal sermon was built around the reality of the resurrection of Christ (Acts 2:23-36). Not only did the message penetrate the hearts of the people; it also became a part of their confession of faith. "If you confess with your mouth, "Jesus is Lord," and *believe in your heart that God raised him from the dead*, you will be saved" (Rom. 10:9).

The message has not changed. The dynamic power still conquers over the fear of death. Truth still assures us that the only triumph over the grave is the living Lord revealed in Scripture. Did he not say, "I am the resurrection and the life. He who *believes* in me will live, even though he dies"? What a truly dynamic message.

A Restless Journey

From the beginning of God's covenant with his people to the concluding verses of *Revelation*, the people of God are always portrayed as being on a journey. We are pilgrims, dwelling in tents, tents which indicate that we are only temporary citizens of this world. But the journey is not easy. Repeatedly in this book I have said that the blessed assurance which we have in Christ does not eliminate the possibility of sorrow or suffering. Conflict at times becomes inevitable. As pilgrims we experience both blessings and burdens.

Those who witnessed the Resurrection and courageously shared the good news with others found themselves faced by persecution. Their journey was far from peaceful. "Some faced jeers and flogging, while still others were chained and put in prison. They were stoned; they were sawed in two; they were put to death by the sword. They went about in sheepskins and goatskins, destitute, persecuted and mistreated—the world was not worthy of them" (Heb. 11:36-38).

Where, you ask, was the joy and hope spoken of in Scripture and in this book? The joy and hope were present in the reality that there is nothing in this life or the next that can defeat you. The Christian wins either way. To remain in this life, faced by suffering, is to know that Christ is with you, for Christ never leaves or forsakes his own. Or, to depart and be with the Lord reveals that where Jesus is, it's heaven there.

It is a restless journey, one that tests your faith and drives you to your knees, but the ultimate victory is assured by the risen Lord. Though the journey is rough and steep, the Pioneer of our faith has given us a word for the journey: "Whoever lives and believes in me shall never die." And when it becomes too restless, you hear him say, "Peace! be still."

A Faithful Voice

Can you hear God speak in the midst of the storm? You have to listen or all the other sounds drown out his words to you.

Most of us are not very good listeners. We would rather do the speaking by giving our opinion on almost any subject. Death, however, leaves us in silence. We have no comment to make, no answers about why? or where?

Superficially we accept the inevitability of death because Scripture says, "It is appointed . . . once to die" (Heb. 9:27, KJV). The full impact of death with all of its ramifications catches most of us unawares. We become the victims of persons who speculate about life after death but who cannot authenticate the speculative ideas.

At such a time—the time of your death or the death of one you love—you will listen for the sound of *a faithful voice*, one that you have come to know and trust when surrounded by shadows and sorrow. Jesus was *that faithful voice* for Mary and Martha. Lazarus was dead. There appeared to be no hope. Then Jesus spoke and reality was experienced, a reality that helped them to know that Jesus, by the sound of his voice, called Lazarus forth from the tomb.

On Easter Sunday, 1979, James W. Angell, Pastor of Claremont Presbyterian Church in Claremont, California, was awakened by a phone call at 4:45 A.M. The early morning call shattered his world. It seemed that all the lights of his life went out. While driving home from college, Susan, their twenty-one-year-old daughter, had been instantly killed in an automobile accident.

What do you do when your world comes apart? Whose voice do you listen for then? As a Christian family the Angells huddled together and prayed the Lord's Prayer. And out of the discordant sounds of sorrow they heard a faithful voice, as the reality of the resurrected Lord spoke peace to their broken hearts. Pastor Angell writes:

That Easter morning, when life was altered so drastically for us, we went to church as usual. I preached the sermons I had prepared —not to set some example of courage, but to help myself through the morning. To be standing up in front of people I loved, and who loved me, talking about the Resurrection seemed like a more welcome prospect than being closeted at home with a heart doubled up with pain. In spite of this self-serving motivation, the congregation interpreted it as faith translated into action—*words suddenly dressed in reality.*"[2]

Out of his dark despair he heard a faithful voice of one who was real, real enough to walk beside him. And on that morning, Pastor Angell preached on the subject, "On a Clear Day You Can See Forever."

The reality of the Resurrection is not in mystical speculation but in the sound of a faithful voice, assuring you that there is light for your darkness. After the veil is lifted, you can see forever. "In this life," Paul said, "we see through a glass dimly but then face to face."

171

There will be no more sickness, suffering, sorrow, or death because the risen Lord is triumphant. The sound of our loving Lord's faithful voice reassures the believer that because Christ lives, we shall live also.

Michael Faraday, the English physicist, chemist, and physical-chemist, was also a faithful follower of the resurrected Lord. It was not unusual to find him in the regular prayer meeting of the church. During Faraday's final illness, a friend asked him, "What are your speculations now?" Faraday had a thrilling answer. "Speculations," he replied with a bit of a holy boldness, "speculations! I have no speculations, I have certainties. 'I know whom I have believed, and am persuaded that he is able to keep that which I have committed unto him against that day.' "[3]

Yes, this blessed assurance revealed in Scripture is much more than mere speculation. It is the reality that the risen Lord has opened the door to life eternal and abundant. Now you are challenged to reach out by faith, accept his grace, and journey on with him.

Together we have made our pilgrimage through these pages. It is my prayer that you have been conscious of the Holy Spirit guiding us as we have honestly confessed our doubts, explored some new ideas, and deepened our belief in the Word of God. A. W. Tozer, former editor of the *Alliance Weekly*, wrote: "The work of a good book is to incite the reader to moral action, to turn his eyes toward God and urge him forward. Beyond that it cannot go!"[4]

Truly Christ is able to save to the uttermost and to give to you as his child the blessed assurance that all things are possible if you will believe.

Notes

1. Walter Brueggemann, *The Bible Makes Sense* (Atlanta: John Knox Press and Winona, Minn.: Saint Mary's Press, 1977), p. 150.

2. James W. Angell, *Oh Susan!* (Anderson, Ind.: Warner Press, 1973), p. 27.

3. Clovis G. Chappell, *The Road to Certainty* (Nashville: Cokesbury Press, 1940), p. 84-85.

4. A. W. Tozer (compiled by G. B. Smith), *Renewed Day by Day* (Camp Hill, Pa.: Christian Publications, Inc., 1980), Preface.

Blessed Assurance
As Revealed in Scripture
Chapter 12
The Resurrection Is for Real!

Resurrection Revealed

Matthew 16:21

From that time on Jesus began to explain to his disciples that he must go to Jerusalem and suffer many things at the hands of the elders, chief priests and teachers of the law, and that he must be killed and on the third day be raised to life.

Matthew 22:30-32

At the resurrection people will neither marry nor be given in marriage; they will be like the angels in heaven. But about the resurrection of the dead—have you not read what God said to you, "I am the God of Abraham, the God of Isaac, and the God of Jacob"? He is not the God of the dead but of the living.

Mark 8:31

He then began to teach them that the Son of Man must suffer many things and be rejected by the elders, chief priests and teachers of the law, and that he must be killed and after three days rise again.

Mark 9:9-10

As they were coming down the mountain, Jesus gave them orders not to tell anyone what they had seen until the Son of Man had risen from the dead. They kept the matter to themselves, discussing what "rising from the dead" meant.

Mark 9:31
He said to them, "The Son of Man is going to be betrayed into the hands of men. They will kill him, and after three days he will rise."

Mark 10:33-34
"We are going up to Jerusalem," he said, "and the Son of Man will be betrayed to the chief priests and teachers of the law. They will condemn him to death and will hand him over to the Gentiles, who will mock him and spit on him, flog him and kill him. Three days later he will rise."

Mark 14:28
But after I have risen, I will go ahead of you into Galilee.

Luke 14:14
And you will be blessed. Although they cannot repay you, you will be repaid at the resurrection of the righteous.

Luke 18:33
On the third day he will rise again.

Luke 20:35-38
But those who are considered worthy of taking part in that age and in the resurrection from the dead will neither marry nor be given in marriage, and they can no longer die; for they are like the angels. They are God's children, since they are children of the resurrection. But in the account of the bush, even Moses showed that the dead rise, for he calls the Lord "the God of Abraham, and the God of Isaac, and the God of Jacob." He is not the God of the dead, but of the living, for to him all are alive.

John 11:25

Jesus said to her, "I am the resurrection and the life. He who believes in me will live, even though he dies; and whoever lives and believes in me will never die."

Acts 26:22-23

But I have had God's help to this very day, and so I stand here and testify to small and great alike. I am saying nothing beyond what the prophets and Moses said would happen—that the Christ would suffer and, as the first to rise from the dead, would proclaim light to his own people and to the Gentiles.

Resurrection Realized

Matthew 28:5-7

The angel said to the women, "Do not be afraid, for I know that you are looking for Jesus, who was crucified. He is not here; he has risen, just as he said. Come and see the place where he lay. Then go quickly and tell his disciples: 'He has risen from the dead and is going ahead of you into Galilee, There you will see him.' Now I have told you."

Mark 16:6

"Don't be alarmed," he said. "You are looking for Jesus the Nazarene, who was crucified. He has risen! He is not here. See the place where they laid him."

Luke 24:6-8

He is not here; he has risen! Remember how he told you, while he was still with you in Galilee: "The Son of Man must be delivered into the hands of sinful men, be crucified and on the third day be raised again." Then they remembered his words.

Luke 24:34

It is true! The Lord has risen and has appeared to Simon.

John 20:17

Jesus said, "Do not hold on to me, for I have not yet returned to the Father. Go instead to my brothers and tell them, 'I am returning to my Father and your Father, to my God and your God.' "

Romans 1:2-4

The gospel he promised beforehand through his prophets in the Holy Scriptures regarding his Son, who as to his human nature was a descendant of David, and who through the Spirit of holiness was declared with power to be the Son of God by his resurrection from the dead: Jesus Christ our Lord.

1 Corinthians 15:3-8

For what I received I passed on to you as of first importance: that Christ died for our sins according to the Scriptures, that he was buried, that he was raised on the third day according to the Scriptures, and that he appeared to Peter, and then to the Twelve. After that, he appeared to more than five hundred of the brothers at the same time, most of whom are still living, though some have fallen asleep. Then he appeared to James, then to all the apostles, and last of all he appeared to me also, as to one abnormally born.

Resurrection Results

John 20:19-20

On the evening of that first day of the week, when the disciples were together, with the doors locked for fear of the Jews, Jesus came and stood among them and said, "Peace be with you!" After he said this, he showed them his hands and side. The disciples were overjoyed when they saw the Lord.

John 20:26-28

A week later his disciples were in the house again, and Thomas was with them. Though the doors were locked, Jesus came and stood among them and said, "Peace be with you!" Then he said to Thomas, "Put your finger here; see my hands. Reach out your hand and put it into my side. Stop doubting and believe."

Thomas said to him, "My Lord and my God!"

Acts 2:32

God has raised this Jesus to life, and we are all witnesses of the fact.

Acts 4:2

They were greatly disturbed because the apostles were teaching the people and proclaiming in Jesus the resurrection of the dead.

Acts 4:33

With great power the apostles continued to testify to the resurrection of the Lord Jesus, and much grace was with them all.

Romans 6:4-5

We were therefore buried with him through baptism into death in order that, just as Christ was raised from the dead through the glory of the Father, we too may live a new life.

If we have been united with him in his death, we will certainly also be united with him in his resurrection.

1 Corinthians 15:21-22

For since death came through a man, the resurrection of the dead comes also through a man. For as in Adam all die, so in Christ all will be made alive.

1 Corinthians 15:51-52

Listen, I tell you a mystery: We will not all sleep, but we will all be changed—in a flash, in the twinkling of an eye, at the last trumpet. For the trumpet will sound, the dead will be raised imperishable, and we will be changed.

1 Thessalonians 4:16-17

For the Lord himself will come down from heaven, with a loud command, with the voice of the archangel and with the trumpet call of God, and the dead in Christ will rise first. After that, we who are still alive and are left will be caught up with them in the clouds to meet the Lord in the air. And so we will be with the Lord forever.

Resurrection Realities

John 14:1-3

Do not let your hearts be troubled. Trust in God; trust also in me. In my Father's house are many rooms; if it were not so, I would have told you. I am going there to prepare a place for you. And if I go and prepare a place for you, I will come back and take you to be with me that you also may be where I am.

John 21:12-14

Jesus said to them, "Come and have breakfast." None of the disciples dared ask him, "Who are you?" They knew it was the Lord. Jesus came, took the bread and gave it to them, and did the same with the fish. This was now the third time Jesus appeared to his disciples after he was raised from the dead.

Acts 2:31-33

Seeing what was ahead, he spoke of the resurrection of the Christ, that he was not abandoned to the grave, nor did his body see decay. God has raised this Jesus to life, and we are all witnesses of the fact. Exalted to the right hand of God, he has received from the Father the promised Holy Spirit and has poured out what you now see and hear.

Acts 2:36

Therefore let all Israel be assured of this: God has made this Jesus, whom you crucified, both Lord and Christ.

Acts 17:30-31

In the past God overlooked such ignorance, but now he commands all people everywhere to repent. For he has set a day when he will judge the world with justice by the man he has appointed. He has given proof of this to all men by raising him from the dead.

Philippians 3:10-11

I want to know Christ and the power of his resurrection and the fellowship of sharing in his sufferings, becoming like him in his death, and so, somehow, to attain to the resurrection from the dead.

1 Peter 1:3

Praise be to the God and Father of our Lord Jesus Christ! In his great mercy he has given us new birth into a living hope through the resurrection of Jesus Christ from the dead.

1 Peter 3:21-22

And this water symbolizes baptism that now saves you also—not the removal of dirt from the body but the pledge of a good conscience toward God. It saves you by the resurrection of Jesus Christ, who has gone into heaven and is at God's right hand—with angels, authorities and powers in submission to him.

Revelation 20:12-13

And I saw the dead, great and small, standing before the throne, and books were opened. Another book was opened, which is the book of life. The dead were judged according to what they had done as recorded in the books. The sea gave up the dead that were in it, and death and Hades gave up the dead that were in them, and each person was judged according to what he had done.

Revelation 21:1-4

Then I saw a new heaven and a new earth, for the first heaven and the first earth had passed away, and there was no longer any sea. I saw the Holy City, the new Jerusalem, coming down out of heaven from God, prepared as a bride beautifully dressed for her husband. And I heard a loud voice from the throne saying, "Now the dwelling of God is with men, and he will live with them. They will be his people, and God himself will be with them and be their God. He will wipe every tear from their eyes.

There will be no more death or mourning or crying or pain, for the old order of things has passed away."